D0203965

THE MARGINAL WORLD OF
WORLD OF
Ōe
Kenzaburo

An East Gate Book

THE MARGINAL WORLD OF

Ōe Kenzaburo

A Study in Themes and Techniques

Michiko N. Wilson

M. E. Sharpe, Inc.

ARMONK, NEW YORK/LONDON

In memory of
Victor Turner
1920–1983

East Gate Books are edited by Douglas Merwin
120 Buena Vista Drive, White Plains, New York 10603

Available in the United Kingdom and Europe from M. E. Sharpe, Publishers, 3 Henrietta Street, London WC2E 8 LU.

Library of Congress Cataloging in Publication Data

Wilson, Michiko N.
    The marginal world of Ōe Kenzaburō.
    Bibliography: p.
    Includes index.
    1. Ōe, Kenzaburō, 1935-   —Criticism and interpretation.
I. Ōe, Kenzaburō, 1935-   . II. Title.
PL858.E14Z98   1986   895.6'35   85-22150
ISBN 0-87332-343-2

Printed in the United States of America

Contents

Preface

"His peculiar synthesis of innocent eye and sophisticated brain," the late Victor Turner said of Ōe Kenzaburo, "has a prophetic thrust which few novelists today, including Saul Bellow and Gabriel García Márquez, can rival in posing uniquely modern problems and demolishing uniquely modern idols." To place the narratives of this creative mind in the mainstream of world literature is my primary concern in this study. Ōe clearly stands at the juncture of modern Japanese and Western literary traditions. It is refreshing to see how he is totally at ease with a variety of Western intellectual and literary disciplines without sacrificing his Japanese identity.

A treasure-trove for literary critics, Ōe's narratives cultivate various foreign and indigenous devices that entice both the reader and the critic to look at literature from an entirely new angle. For me, the formalist/structuralist approach is most exciting and rewarding in dealing with Ōe's marginal world. At the same time, I find it essential to analyze his work in terms of the relationship of one narrative to another. My particular focus is to unravel the characteristics of his art and the power of narrative discourse. I hope that this introductory study will stimulate further discussion and translation of his provocative and creative achievements.

Unless designated otherwise, all quotations of Ōe's narratives are my translations. When another English translation is available, the first number in a bracket after each quotation indicates the number in the original text; the second, the number in the translation. For Japanese names, I follow the Japanese custom of putting the surname first, given name second. The place of publication for all the Japanese books cited is Tokyo. An earlier version of chapter 7 appeared in *The Journal of Japanese Studies* 7, 1 (Winter 1981), under the title "Ōe's Obsessive Metaphor, Mori the Idiot Son: Toward the Imagination of Satire, Regeneration, and Grotesque Realism." For permission to reprint it in a revised and enlarged form I would like to thank the editor.

I am profoundly indebted to Mr. Ōe Kenzaburo for kindly providing me with various materials for my research and, more than anything else, for inspiring me to undertake this project. I wish to thank Kenny Marotta, who offered extremely helpful criticism of the manuscript's style chapter by chapter with patience, insight, and understanding. His assistance was indispensable to the completion of this study. My thanks are also due to Mary McKinley, Janet A. Walker, Keiko McDonald, and Mohammad Ghanoonparvar, who gave me valuable suggestions and constant encouragement. For their perceptive appreciation of Ōe's genius, I am most grateful to the late Victor Turner and to his wife, Edith, with whom I have had many delightful discussions on the subject. My thanks also go to Cynthia Ingraham, who took time to proofread the entire manuscript; Mildred Nuechterlein, who typed the final draft; and John Tongate and Ira Carver at the Perry-Castañeda Library of the University of Texas, who accommodated me in my research and writing for part of the book. I also owe appreciation to Alfred MacAdam for his support and advice. I am grateful to the University of Virginia for two summer research fellowships and a Sesquicentennial Associateship, which enabled me to devote my time entirely to the book. Finally, I would like to acknowledge my debt to my husband, Michael, for his editorial suggestions and unwavering support.

M.N.W.

THE MARGINAL WORLD OF
WORLD OF
Ōe
Kenzaburo

1

Introduction

Although the narratives of Ōe Kenzaburo (1935–) are deeply rooted in the indigenous culture of Japan, they are ultimately concerned with what is uniquely literary, not with what is uniquely Japanese. In this sense his narratives are "transcultural and transhistoric"[1] to the core. In scope of vision, breadth of subject matter, and brilliance of artistic imagination and experimentation, no other Japanese writer equals Ōe.[2]

In a lecture delivered to the first Japanese Semiotics Conference held in August 1981, Ōe humorously meddled with the ending of Shiga Naoya's (1833–1971) *A Dark Night's Passing* (Anya kōro, 1937), regarded as a masterpiece and a model of "pure literature" (*jun bungaku*).[3] After Ōe links semiotically the protagonist's anxiety over his wife's adultery with an appearance of a flying object (an airplane), he calls attention to the way Shiga concludes the novel: the protagonist climbs a mountain, experiences the suffering of life and near-death, and comes one step closer to self-salvation. Just before the climb, he has a severe bout of diarrhea. He stops it artificially by taking a heavy dose of herbal medicine. In the mountain he feels his physical exhaustion turning into rapture, his mind and body merging into the great bounty of nature that surrounds him. After the climb, he develops intestinal catarrh and goes into delirium. Ōe emphasizes two points: (1) the protagonist dissolves the confrontation between nature and himself by merging into nature, and (2) the novel "does not end with Tokitō Kensaku gaining self reliance and moving into new territory."[4] Here,

Ōe raises an issue never voiced by any of his predecessors or contemporaries: "Wasn't there another way of ending the novel? If there were, Japanese literature would have taken a slightly different course."[5]

To illustrate a different ending to *A Dark Night's Passing*, Ōe brings in semiotics, specifically the concept of "grotesque realism" put forward by Mikhail M. Bakhtin in his famous Rabelais discussion. Based on the image system of carnivalization in Europe, one of the images of "grotesque realism" deals with human excrement. Central to Bakhtin's analysis is the ambivalent nature of excrement. In ancient scatological images, excrement is "linked to the generating force and to fertility. On the other hand, excrement is conceived as something *intermediate between earth and body*, as something relating the one to the other. It is also an intermediate between the living body and dead, disintegrating matter that is being transformed into the earth, into manure. The living body returns to the earth its excrement, which fertilizes the earth as does the body of the dead."[6] Possessing this dynamic element, excrement plays the key role in Ōe's version of how to end *A Dark Night's Passing*: "Shiga Naoya did not have to make Tokitō Kensaku take the herbal medicine. He could have come up with another solution: let Kensaku continue his bout with the diarrhea. For example, let us say Kensaku runs around [on the mountain] with diarrhea. He shits all over the place. . . . Through this, a dynamic regeneration takes place. Rather than letting him merge into nature, and dissolving the confrontation between him and nature, Shiga could have regenerated Tokitō Kensaku as a character who actively interacts with nature. Had he concluded *A Dark Night's Passing* with the [alternate] ending, would not Japanese literature have changed a little?"[7]

The usual approach to fiction in Japan tacitly but doggedly assumes that "in the process of writing a novel, there is actually no need, at a conscious level, to use a mechanism or methodological device."[8] Ōe makes a radical break with this conventional wisdom exercised by the still popular "I-novel" (*shishōsetsu*), whose most consummate artist is Shiga Naoya. What the definition of this traditional fiction exactly is still generates debate among critics.[9] It is commonly held that the "I-novel" records and exposes the writer's candid emotions, failures, and lifestyle, i.e., his "undisguised personal preliterary self" in the manner of a narrative.[10] Its viewpoint is inevitably confined to the writer's limited environment as it replaces "the pluralist 'real world' with a private universe."[11] Based on the fusion or confusion of art and life, the solemn tone of the "I-novel" leaves hardly any room for humor, imagination, and experimentation. In fact, one critic goes so far as to say that this autobiographical novel is "the essential pattern of Japanese prose fiction toward which even the most panoramic social novel gravitates."[12] One of the most popular yet controversial novelists in Japan, Ōe openly questions the historical concept of autobiographical fiction, *shishōsetsu*, because it "stoically restrains the function of imagination" as it binds the protagonist "I" to the everyday environment.[13]

Shiga Naoya wrote *A Dark Night's Passing* without any conscious literary device, thereby establishing a *modus operandi* for the writer in Japan that stressed the production of antimethodological novels. According to the "dictates" of the god of "pure literature," the writer should strive for clear, one-dimensional sentences, never polysemic ones. On the contrary, Ōe argues, literature depends on the very creation of a kind of electric transformer that changes polysemic reality to fiction while still employing language that is one-dimensional. "This transformer is a device of literary expression [i.e., poetic language contrasted with everyday language]. This is what I mean by creating literature, creating fiction."[14]

Under the influence of the works of Russian semioticians, notably those of Yurij M. Lotman as well as Bakhtin, Ōe has stated repeatedly the inadequacy of the kind of personal, confessional writing advocated by his predecessors:

> As long as the reality we live in has an obscure, multifaceted appearance, narrative representation by means of traditional, one-dimensional descriptions is no match for reality. Therefore, by setting up various devices in narrative discourse, we must present expressions that can cope with the multifacetedness of reality. This is the gist of what semioticians are saying. One of the characteristics of contemporary literature is that, by linking various levels [of reality], it expresses reality, not one-dimensionally, but by extending itself to the human psyche within and without. To that end, we must chisel out different levels and strata. These levels and strata sometimes constitute different times, sometimes different places. Or, different levels and strata of human consciousness. We must distinguish one level from another, one stratum from another, and at the same time must synthesize them into a wholeness to organize a novel. In other words, we need to invent something that connects all the multiformed strata.[15]

Lotman views literature "as an intricate modeling system that is an analogue to complex phenomena of life'' and also ''as a special kind of system of signs.''[16] His theory of art as a model serves to validate Ōe's belief in the similarity between art and life: created by synthesis, art models both reality and an artist's own consciousness. This structure of reality that the artist creates in turn affects him. ''But since the work itself is, once created, a part of reality, it can influence the perception . . . of the perceiver. Thus the interaction of art and life is a spiralling process or movable correlation.''[17]

Writing in the simplest of narrative forms, Ōe began his career with certain images, interests, topics, and obsessions that continue to appear in his latest works. These raw data—his childhood in a village on Shikoku, the defeat of Japan, the figure of the divine Emperor, the specter of the A-bomb, and the birth of his retarded son—have continuously intermeshed with Ōe's art, as they grow increasingly complex in his later works. That his narratives model both reality and his own consciousness, that his own structure of reality affects him, is clearly stated in a 1976 essay: ''The birth of the handicapped first baby in my real life has continuously influenced my fictional world long after the composition of *A Personal Matter* [Kojinteki na taiken, 1964]. If I had not existed in this real world, my son would not be here. But, on the other hand, if he were not here, I could not be living the way I am. At the time of his birth . . . in the midst of confusion and commotion, as I almost prepared both birth and death certificates, I let my instinct have its way and named the boy Hikari [light]. My instinct was right. His existence has since illuminated the dark, deep folds of my consciousness as well as its bright sides.''[18]

This type of raw material would have tempted many Japanese writers to produce the ''I-novel.''[19] However, Ōe learned to transform experiential material into an artistic experience that releases both the writer and the reader from reality's limitations, and, in Ōe's words, activates man in his entirety.

> I have written a lot about the physical abnormality of my child and his retardation. However, I have not done so in the manner of the ''I-novel.'' . . . I am the father of a brain-damaged child, and I have written stories about him, but I have not presented him as I would in an ''I-novel.'' His existence in real life continues to make various kinds of impacts on me. To live in this world, for me, is to live with him. What these impacts had produced, what was at the core of our communal life—only when these things became *imaginatively independent* and came out of my interiority, did I write about him.

> I live in this cosmos-world-society as a human being. This child of mine deeply and sharply influences the structure of my flesh and spirit. Therefore, when I write about trees and whales, these words, which embody symbolic meanings, constantly reflect the shadow of the child's existence. Conversely, I write about the idiot infant. The words that describe him, however, do not portray the retarded child who exists in my own family. My words . . . like a surrealist painting that places the sky and an ocean in the orifices of a human body, are the *very image of this cosmos-world-society* which I glimpse through the flesh and spirit of the idiot child.[20]

What is at work in this re-creation of reality, the reflection of Ōe's retarded son, is the notion that considers imagination to be the faculty of deforming images offered by perception, of freeing ourselves from our immediate images, rather than of forming images: it is "especially the faculty of *changing* of images. If there is not a changing of images, an unexpected union of images, there is no imagination, no *imaginative* action. If a *present* image does not recall an *absent* one, if an occasional image does not give rise to a swarm of aberrant images, to an explosion of images, there is no imagination."[21]

As a novice writer, Ōe was not yet familiar with Bachelard's revolutionary concept of imagination. Neither was he aware of the trickster theory, the cultural hero, the archetype of a clown, which supports the aesthetics of his later novels. Another aesthetic concept, "grotesque realism," did not enter his literary universe until after the completion of *The Waters Have Come in unto My Soul* (Kōzui wa waga tamashii ni oyobi, 1973).[22] However, in his psyche and his imagination there always resided the germ of all these ideas formulated by scholars of psychoanalysis, anthropology, folklore, mythology, and literary theory. In a sense these scholars have indirectly served Ōe, who needed a theoretical basis for his literary formulations. We might say that the encounter with their works is a rediscovery as well as a learning process for him.

When he began to write short stories at the age of twenty-two, stories that focused on college students who take part-time jobs killing dogs kept for experiments ("A Strange Job" [Kimyō na shigoto], 1957), or transferring corpses at a university hospital ("Lavish Are the Dead" [Shisha no ogori], 1957),[23] deformation of images was already his essential methodology. Whether he dealt with the child/infant in a village community or youths in postwar Japan, his characters play the role of outsiders who occupy the periphery of a society. Many years later he was introduced to Victor Turner's theory of "liminality" in the ritual process and the marginal world of "communitas," which firmly reassured the Japanese novelist of the validity of his own literary experimentations.[24] Marginality always subsumes something dangerous or even subversive. If his early stories contained the belligerent, subversive elements of Norman Mailer or Henry Miller, this fact originated in the spirit of "grotesque realism" and "communitas," the debasement and degradation in laughter, rather than the political imagination of a revolution. If, from the earliest works on, Ōe revealed the vitality of Rabelaisian comedy or slapstick farce sometimes verging on literary obscenity, this tendency has everything to do with his inborn skill as a clown.[25]

"The writer's job is the job of a clown," Ōe insists, "the clown who also talks about sorrow."[26] It is also to make a "violent, urgent confession through language and imagination." And, as Blake put it, this imagination is "not a State: it is the Human Existence itself,"[27] which extends to the cosmos-world-society. The writer/clown participates, through laughter and tears, in the ceaseless flow of reality, constantly thinking of the present in light of the past; his role inevitably contains an element of subversion.[28] "The writer confronts the real world head-on. He seems to be even blocking the advance of the real world. It is in this sense that the words of imagination become his only weapon in the struggle to overcome and deny the real world."[29]

An important word implied here is "commitment": Ōe is a committed writer, socially and politically, his articulateness on political and social issues being a cause of bafflement for Japanese literary critics. By "politically," I have in mind Norman Mailer's definition of "politics" as an integral part of man as a social being, politics "as a part of everything else in life."[30] Ōe, who began his career to "succeed to the legacy left by postwar writers," also faced the no-choice situation of being a writer in the Nuclear Age. The terror of nuclear war, inseparable from his consciousness, is linked to the eschatological vision that arches over his work and his real life. "I know very little about the Bible," he once wrote, "but the gods who deluged the earth must have calculated on Noah's capability of restoring the human world before they sent the flood. Had Noah turned out to be a sluggard, a hysterical Jeremiah with no ability to restore the world, and had the postdeluvian world continued to be a wasteland, it would have certainly caused consternation among the gods in the heavens. . . . The atomic bomb that devastated Hiroshima was the worst deluge in the twentieth century. Amidst the great flood the people of Hiroshima immediately began to restore their world. By saving themselves, they also saved the souls of those who dropped the A-bomb. In the current deluge that we are faced with, the cosmic deluge frozen at this moment, yet ready to melt and engulf us at any time, the souls which the people of Hiroshima have saved include all the souls of humanity in the twentieth century earth seized with the cancer called 'the possession of nuclear armaments.' ''[31]

Speaking to a crowd of specialists at the Conference on Asian Peace Research in a Global Context, Ōe again reaffirmed his role as a trickster under the nuclear threat who ''at once agitates and activates the conference that explores a consistent, if not systematized, theme.''[32] ''The writer keeps saying to every specialist: You are an insider, or you have at least the potential to become an insider unawares, to confront the masses who are outsiders. You might say that the writer, by saying so, continues at the same time to confirm his position as an outsider. In this respect he resembles a clown at a royal court. Faced with power or anything linked to it, the clown, relying on his status as an outsider, raises questions, criticizes them, and laughs at everything under the sun. He in turn cannot escape being laughed at. This is the kind of clown's role I would like to assume as a writer.''[33] This writer/clown, however, can so far utter only shrieks of terror rather than laugh at nuclear power. Ōe points out that there is a positive side to the shrieks that are transmitted through language. He again bases his argument on Lotman's art model theory: the writer/clown makes a model of the time he lives in, and communicates with ordinary people. If the model is rooted in folk culture, his outcries are the very expression of the hope for regeneration, which surmounts the worst, most deadly situation of all, the nuclear threat.[34]

One such writer/clown with whom Ōe feels kindship is a Korean poet, Kim Chi Ha, whose poetic imagination has continuously made an impact on Ōe in his commitment to communicate with the people of his time.[35] ''Kim Chi Ha, who regards the people's culture as the source of his poetic imagination, is encouraging us to rediscover a cultural force, which Japan has lost in the process of modernization, within the Japanese folk culture, a force that generates . . . 'grotesque realism' that laughs at everything, including himself, or death which is closely linked with rebirth, or the continual *reversal* of rigidly fixed hierarchical relationships.''[36]

On the ultimate question, of what use is art, Ōe calls attention to another humanist whom he sees as his fellow traveller on the other side of the Pacific Ocean, Kurt Vonnegut, who is as vociferous as Ōe in protecting the "lovely blue green planet" from nuclear disaster. Ōe's American contemporary offers what he calls "the canary in the coal mine theory of arts." "This theory," Vonnegut said in a meeting of physics teachers, "says that artists are useful to society because they are so sensitive. They are super-sensitive. They keel over like canaries in poison coal mines long before more robust types realize that there is any danger whatsoever. The most useful thing I could do before this meeting today is to keel over right now. On the other hand, artists are keeling over by the thousands every day and nobody seems to pay the least attention."[37] Fragility and sensitivity, the shrieks of terror and the laughter through language, these are the only weapons a writer possesses. The work of art he creates is nothing more than a fragile attempt to discover a way by which a human being can outgrow a maddening situation created by the contemporary world, a situation wherein "the briefest fit of stupidity could easily guarantee the end of the world."[38] What Ōe the writer/clown ultimately wants to express is "the voice of Man" that echoes in the past, present, and future, repeating the words, "O teach us to outgrow our madness," O teach us to outgrow our nuclear age, save our planet, trees, whales and humans. "Till they construct at last a human justice/The contribution of our star, within the shadow/Of which uplifting, loving, and constraining power/All other reasons may rejoice and operate.'"[39]

*   *   *

Ōe's complex narrative devices prove to be a constant challenge to the reader and critic. His later works, in particular, lead us to a fundamental question: In what respects is a literary work different from other humanistic products? He defines a novel as "the device made by language to activate man in his entirety."[40] According to this definition, it is not the job of literary criticism to transpose a literary work to another type of discourse, as is traditionally done, but to "study the underlying properties of literary discourse itself."[41] "To consider the method of a novel," Ōe tells us, "means to investigate the mechanisms and workings of the verbal device . . . the method of a novel has a structure, and this structure is multilayered."[42] For example, one of the useful ways to investigate the mechanisms at work in Ōe's narratives is to recognize the two essential elements that make up a literary text: "story" and "discourse." First identified by Russian formalists, later elaborated by French structuralists, *story* ("what") refers to a presentation of phenomena that occurred at a certain time without the speaker's intervention in the events reported.[43] This is also what Gérard Genette calls "narrative content" regardless of its low dramatic intensity or fullness of incident.[44] On the other hand, *narrative discourse* ("how") refers to any speech act that presupposes a speaker and a listener, the former with an intention to influence the latter. What counts here is the manner in which the narrator recounts the events, how he confronts the reader who perceives them.[45] Genette designates this as statement, discourse, or the narrative text itself.

In analyzing, from a writer's viewpoint, Faulkner—the most provocative writer among the English and Americans for Ōe—he pleads with the reader/critic: "I have long hoped that literature specialists would show us a kind of reading based on methodology. This is because I am fully convinced from my own experience that, in a verbal art like the novel, reading the mechanism of expressions, i.e., a methodological reading, offers the most positive way of reading the novel. I also believe that a methodological reading conducted by specialists has an educational use for the general reader, which in turn helps me to take one step forward in my creative writing. One of the few fields that offers a happy domain to be shared by specialists, consumers, and producers is, I believe, literature."[46] A "structuralist" view implied in the kind of reading to which Ōe calls our attention aims at a synthesis, an activation of man in his entire being, seeking to "link to history not only certain contents . . . but also certain forms, not only the material but also the intelligible, not only the ideological but also the aesthetic."[47] It is in this sense that the reader can grasp a novel that corresponds to the polysemy of reality, a novel in which the writer "directs his efforts, as much as possible, towards making various humanistic elements into a whole."[48]

2

The Adventures of Two Brothers: Linking the Novel and Reality

Ōe's first works (written in 1957) portrayed his contemporaries—the college youth of the 1950s. He then immediately shifted his attention to the primordial world of the child/infant. "Prize Stock" (Shiiku, 1958) introduces for the first time "the village in the valley" on Shikoku, the birth place of two young brothers. "My kid brother and I were digging with pieces of wood in the loose earth that smelled of fat and ashes at the surface of the crematorium, the makeshift crematorium in the valley that was simply a shallow pit in a clearing in the underbrush. The valley bottom was already wrapped in the dusk and fog as cold as the spring water that welled up in the woods, but the side of the hill where we lived, the little village built around a cobblestone road, was bathed in grape light. I straightened out of a crouch and weakly yawned, my mouth stretching open. My brother stood up too, gave a small yawn and smiled at me" (101/113).[1] Thus opens the story that won the coveted Akutagawa Prize. An Edenic land protected by a virgin forest, the little summer village in the valley no longer exists for the two brothers after the summer of 1945.[2]

This image of the two young brothers, of the child/infant, became an important literary device for Ōe. He explained the significance of the device twenty years later: "Methodologically speaking, I began to write novels quite unconsciously. However, from my early works on, it is clear that the child/infant has played a methodological role as a positive element."[3] In his discussion of the "child motif," Ōe draws upon the psychological-mythological analyses of the child archetype presented by C. G. Jung and C. Kerényi. Jung defines the child motif in mythology as one that "represents the pre-conscious, childhood aspect of the collective psyche."[4] Kerényi notes that, usually an "abandoned foundling," the child god is often threatened by extraordinary dangers.

Jung enumerates four characteristic elements of the child god: abandonment, invincibility, hermaphroditism, and the child as beginning and end. The "child's" insignificant beginnings and its mysterious and miraculous birth are characterized by abandonment, exposure, and danger (p. 5). "Out of this situation 'child' emerges as a symbolic content, manifestly separated or even isolated from its background (the mother), but sometimes including the mother in its perilous situation" (p. 87). Since "child" means something evolving toward independence, a "nascent whole," or on the way to wholeness, the detachment from its origins, abandonment, is a "necessary condition." At the same time, "child" possesses powers "far exceeding those of ordinary humanity," and despite all dangers, will survive. Jung also tells us that " 'child' is born out of the depths of human nature, or rather out of living Nature herself. It is a personification of vital forces quite outside the limited range of our conscious mind, of ways and possibilities of which our one-sided conscious mind knows nothing; a wholeness which embraces the very depths of Nature" (p. 89).

The child as the hermaphrodite, representing a "union of the strongest and most striking opposites," becomes a "subduer of conflicts and a bringer of healing." It spans a bridge between "present-day consciousness, always in danger of losing its roots, and the natural, unconscious, instinctive wholeness of primeval times" (p. 93). As the "bisexual primordial being," the "child" turns into "a symbol of the unity of personality, a symbol of the self, where the war of opposites finds peace" (p. 94). Finally, the "child," being *renatus in novam*, means "both beginning and end, an initial and a terminal creature. The initial creature existed before man was, and the terminal creature will be when man is not" (p. 97). The "child" had a psychic life before it had its consciousness; it symbolizes the "pre-conscious and the post-conscious essence of man."

Of these four elements of the "child archetype," "Prize Stock" and *Nip the Buds, Gun the Kids* (Memushiri kouchi, 1958, hereafter *Nip the Buds*) deal primarily with the abandonment and the hermaphroditism of the child/infant. "When I was groping my way along as a novice writer," Ōe wrote, "I repeatedly characterized the child/infant as an 'abandoned foundling.' . . . As long as he was born out of the unconscious, he was delivered into this world as if he were a plaything. If that is the case, he might also be destroyed like a plaything."[5] Ōe's "abandoned foundling," exposed to dangers, is also a "bisexual primordial being": "I placed at the pivot of the [narrative] structure a young boy as 'the older brother,' and an infant as 'the younger brother.' This 'younger brother' was often the existence that manifested the 'hermaphroditism' for 'the older brother.' "[6]

*   *   *

"Prize Stock" relates through the older brother's eyes the capture of an American black soldier whose plane has been shot down at the end of the war. The narrator's father, who has been entrusted with the job of keeping the black soldier (called the "catch") alive, eventually lets the narrator take care of the "catch" in the cellar. Like the "hunting dogs and the children and the trees," the black soldier, "a gentle animal," becomes a "component of village life." United by "a sudden, deep, passionate bond that was almost 'human,' " the narrator, his brother, and their best friend, Harelip, communicate with the black soldier without the means of spoken language. Finally a messenger from the "town," Clerk, brings the verdict on the fate of the "catch": the prisoner must be handed over to the army. The narrator's frantic gestures, filled with fright and desperation that warn the black soldier of the transfer, provoke the "catch" to hold the boy hostage in the cellar. The adults break in; the narrator's father with a hatchet, smashes the skull of the black soldier, who is about to strangle the boy. Unfortunately, in the ensuing struggle, the boy's left hand is mutilated.

"Prize Stock" also tells the story of the dissolution of the Arcadian world in the village in the valley, of two young brothers growing up, and of the war experienced by the child/infant. The narrative, opening with the words "My kid brother and I" and ending with the words "I went down the grassy slope to look for my brother" (138/168), reveals Ōe's "unconscious methodological" exercise in exploring the primordial world of the child/infant. In the center of this world is the "catch," "a black horse, full and beautiful," worshipped by the village children. The narrator recounts a ritual, "an archaic bathing in the spring," that is performed to celebrate the unprecedented summer and the miraculous presence of the black soldier.

> When we were as naked as birds and had stripped the black soldier's clothes we plunged into the spring altogether, splashing one another and shouting. We were enraptured with our new idea. . . . We clamored around him splashing and shouting, and by and by the girls left the shade of the oak trees where they had been hesitating and came racing into the spring and hurriedly submerged their own small nakedness. Harelip caught one of the girls and began his lewd ritual. . . .
>
> Suddenly we discovered that the black soldier possessed a magnificent, heroic, unbelievably beautiful penis. We crowded around him bumping naked hips, pointing and teasing, and the black soldier gripped his penis and planted his feet apart fiercely like a goat about to copulate and bellowed. We laughed until we cried and splashed the black soldier's penis. (127–8/152)

The black soldier becomes for the young narrator a symbol of the Arcadian world in which man and beasts live happily together: "To us the black soldier was a rare and wonderful domestic animal, an animal of genius. How can I describe how much we loved him, or the blazing sun above our wet, heavy skin that distant, splendid summer afternoon, the deep shadows on the cobblestones, the smell of the children and the black soldier, the voices hoarse with happiness, how can I convey the repletion and rhythm of it all?" (128/153). Here Ōe recaptures the "pre-conscious, childhood aspect of the collective psyche," which leads man back to a wholeness embracing the very depths of Nature. The young narrator instinctively grasps the biological rhythm of primeval times: "To us it seemed that the summer that bared those tough, resplendent muscles, the summer that suddenly and unexpectedly geysered like an oil well, spewing happiness and drenching us in black heavy oil, would continue forever and never end" (128/153).

"Prize Stock" also depicts the relationship of the two brothers as a harmony that remains intact even after the older brother's ordeal as a hostage. His little brother is the only person who can comfort the narrator: "In an awed voice my brother told me repeatedly that he had thought I was dead. For two days I had lain here and eaten nothing and so he had thought I was dead. With my brother's hand on me I entered sleep that lured me as irresistibly as death" (134/162). The younger brother's innocence and maternal gentleness subdue conflicts in the narrator's mind and heal him. When the narrator perceives, however, the significance of this hermaphroditic role his brother plays, the primordial world of childhood no longer belongs to the older brother. He must join the cruel world of adults: "I was no longer a child"

(136/165). With the unconscious replaced by the conscious, the narrator experiences for the first time the pain of war. Clerk unknowingly makes the connection between the end of the Arcadian world and the penetration of the war into the village:

> "When a war starts smashing kids' fingers it's going too far," Clerk said.
> I breathed deeply, and was silent. The war, a long, bloody war on a huge scale, must still have been going on. The war that like a flood washing away flocks of sheep and trimmed lawns in some distant country was never in the world supposed to have reached our village. But it had come, to mash my fingers and hand to a pulp, my father swinging a hatchet, his body drunk on the blood of war. And suddenly our village was enveloped in the war, and in the tumult I could not breathe. (137/166)

In contrast to "Prize Stock," the two brothers in *Nip the Buds*, from the very beginning of the narrative, are placed in the mire of the war. *Nip the Buds* is an account of a group of reform school boys evacuated to a village where a deadly plague has broken out. The villagers flee and abandon the boys. The plague abates, and, when the villagers return, they order the boys to keep silent about their abandonment. The narrator, the leader of the "abandoned foundlings," refuses to acquiesce and escapes into the forest.

Antithetical to the situation in "Prize Stock," there is in *Nip the Buds* no younger brother, no presence of the maternal, primordial, bisexual being, who would heal the pain of the narrator on the run at the end of the story. *Nip the Buds* separates the older brother permanently from his younger sibling. In flashbacks we learn how the younger brother joins the narrator just before the group evacuation. During their abandonment in the village, the younger brother finds a dog who becomes his best friend. Those who have seen the dog dig up a corpse accuse the younger brother of spreading the plague. They blame him for the death of a little girl left behind, whose mother had died in the plague. The older brother is unable to prevent the killing of the dog. In despair, the younger brother runs away and drowns in a flooded river.

The narrator loses both the little girl he came to love and his brother. For the abandoned children, the girl seems to be a sacrificial lamb. "The plague rapidly abated as it plucked the little girl away from me as if to tell me she were the last flower" (297).[7] When the villagers return, they learn that Yi (a Korean boy) has been hiding a deserter. The adults force the young deserter to march "with his innards hanging out," another sacrificial lamb who takes all the blame, woes, and frustrations of the adult world at the end of the war. After the deaths of his brother, his "little lover," and the deserter who nursed the girl day and night, there is no longer any reason for the narrator to remain with the rest of the delinquents, who have in the end betrayed him.

The fifteen juvenile delinquents are children abandoned even by their own parents. For two weeks prior to the group evacuation, the parents were notified to come to pick up their children, but chose to ignore this call to resume the parent-child relationship. During times of massacre society showed such passion, the narrator tells us, incarcerating "young criminals" with records of misdemeanors, or those who supposedly had a predilection to juvenile delinquency. "It was the time of murder. The war like a flood drowned every fold of human sentiment, each and every corner of a body, forests, streets, and the sky with collective madness. Even inside the courtyard of our old brick building where we were detained, all of a sudden a soldier would fall out of the sky, a young blond haired soldier whose buttocks obscenely stuck out of the transparent plane would start firing in confusion. . . . Almost every night, sometimes in broad daylight, the fires caused by air raids lit the sky over the town or smeared it with black smoke" (204–205).

The boys who were the "catch" inside the walls of the reform school are treated by the villagers as "aliens." They are this time inside the "transparent, rubbery thick wall" of the village. However, what we see in the abandoned children is the image of the primordial child/infant in primordial times completely "at home" in the "solitariness of abandonment."[8] A sense of solidarity prevails among the children and they build an autonomous, primeval world. In the face of annihilation by the plague, they join another "abandoned foundling," the Korean boy Yi, and hold a festival in the snow to drive out the evil spirits of the plague.

As is the case with "Prize Stock," what shatters the harmonious world of *Nip the Buds* is the abrupt intervention of adults. The headman entices the hungry boys with the "genuine meal, the humane and abundant meal that was never given to us during our long life in the reform school, the evacuation trip or the time we kids spent alone in the village" (312). The boys desert their leader one by one until the narrator stands alone, abandoned by both adults and children.

> The headman grabbed my chest and almost choked me as he panted with anger.

"Listen, we should strangle a bastard like you while you're still a kid. We crush cripples (*dekizokonai*) while they're babies. We're peasants, we nip the buds that won't grow." . . .

"We can push you off the cliff, we can kill you and nobody'll accuse us of murder.". . .

Scared to death, my comrades kept their mouths shut and betrayed me. . . .

"Hey," the headman said. "Hey, you."

A bad premonition shook me.

"We can kill you, but we'll let you go," said the headman in one breath and peered into my face with eyes that shone darkly. "Get your ass out of here tonight. Get away as far as you can. Remember even if you go to the police, there won't be anybody to testify for you. If you go back to the reform school, you'll be punished for escaping. Don't forget that." (313–4)

Ōe portrays the young narrator as a child exposed and threatened by extraordinary danger. To get out of the village means to commit the prohibited act of escaping; to remain inside the village means imprisonment, possibly death at the hands of the headman. A "lumber lift" is the only way out of the village. The shortcut to the town has been made impassable by a flood, and the lumber lift, suspended over a dark, deep valley, has hauled the children into the village. The same vehicle is about to banish the narrator to another kind of confinement: "I can never escape. Both inside and on the outside tough fingers and powerful arms are patiently waiting to choke and crush me. When the lift stopped, the blacksmith with a weapon in his hand got out first, and I followed. All of a sudden the blacksmith bared his teeth and leapt at me. I lunged forward. The blacksmith's iron bar whistled through the air, barely missing the back of my head. I got up and ran wildly up the dark grove before the iron bar came back at me" (314). Ōe maintains the powerful narrative flow and tension to the very end of the novel, reminding the reader at the same time that *Nip the Buds* is a personal account of the life of the "abandoned foundling": "I was only a child, exhausted, outraged, crying, and trembling from cold and hunger. A wind blew up carrying the approaching footsteps of the villagers. I clenched my teeth and stood up, and ran into the darker clusters of trees, into the thicker underbrush" (315).

*   *   *

As Ōe points out, *Nip the Buds* takes the simplest narrative form: "The novel starts out very simply. On the day of the flood, the first-person narrator [*boku*], the boy who resisted to the end and escaped into the forest, begins his narration about how they, the reform school boys, have come to the village. This is the narrative discourse of the tale. The background is set in one valley. The novel relates what has happened in the village in the valley, and ends when the life of the children in the village ends."[9] Ōe tells us how easy it was for him to write the story: "It had only been thirteen years since the war. The war was deeply tied to my life as if it had ended yesterday. All I had to do was to let my war experiences, not factual but mental, take their own course and write them down."[10]

The simplicity of the narrative discourse of "Prize Stock" and *Nip the Buds* mainly derives from the absence of what Russian formalists call "motivation." Twenty years later, Ōe tried to provide such "motivation" in a sequel to *Nip the Buds* entitled, *The Trial of "Nip the Buds, Gun the Kids"* ("Memushiri kouchi" saiban, 1980, hereafter *The Trial*).[11] This story serves to illustrate the device of "motivation" by which "the very existence of the book is justified in order to make it still 'truer'—it is a manuscript found by chance, a correspondence, or the memoirs of a historical character."[12] *Nip the Buds* and *The Trial* give the reader the opportunity for a fascinating comparative study. When the idea occurred to Ōe that he should rewrite *Nip the Buds* and examine himself as a contemporary writer, he realized that "rewriting the novel required all kinds of devices, which I created energetically. First of all, there is a novelist who wrote *Nip the Buds*. That is to say, he is myself, but therein lies a subtle difference. Therefore, I set up a device to convey the difference. The writer's younger brother sends him a letter from America. And the letter is written in English. In the beginning of the novel, we are told that the novelist is translating the letter into Japanese in his own style. This is what is called 'motivation' " (p. 107).

At the base of the narrative ("how") is the device that the younger brother "speaks" to his brother, the novelist, by means of a letter. It is understood that the older brother wrote *Nip the Buds*, a tale of an accident that actually happened in his own village in the valley. Furthermore, the novelist wrote the story, Ōe explains, "from an outsider's point of view, not from that of the village children. He wrote what is extremely embarrassing to the villagers as if he were accusing them. As a result, he lives in Tokyo as an outcast. And it seems that the village is the same village in *The Game of Contemporaneity* " (p. 107). The story ("what") of *The Trial* concerns another older brother, the protagonist of *Nip the Buds*, who escaped into the forest at the end of the story. He comes back into the village in the valley right after the war, disguised as his own brother who was drowned in the flood. He appears in the village acompanied by American soldiers in a jeep.

While the narrative discourse takes the form of a personal letter, the story unfolds in the form of memoirs that relate how the disguised boy (called "counter-younger brother" [*han-otōto*]) charged the villagers with massacre and put them on trial. "This plot of the Democracy Trial under the leadership of the Occupation army," Ōe remarked, "is well grounded. Of late, the argument that the democracy brought in by the United States in postwar Japan was fake is prevailing. I believe that at least up to 1947 or 1948, the Americans who lived in Japan embodied the remarkable features of democracy, and tried to introduce true democracy" (p. 107).

The trial in Ōe's story consists of two parts, the first part open to all the people in the valley, the second a closed session. The "big shots," participants in the closed trial, transmit its content to the rest of the people. The village actors in turn "dramatize" the trial on the public stage. All of the villagers, adults and children, become both the spectators of and the participants in the festive play that reenacts the trial. However, in the end the false testimony of the "counter-younger brother" falls apart, and he goes with the troops to the United States, where he grows up. To obtain American citizenship, he fights in the Vietnam War, in which he loses his left arm, his right leg, both eyes, a part of his jaw, and his voice. In other words, he embodies the opposite of the beauty his younger brother possessed.

The writer of the narrative text *The Trial*, that is, the younger brother of the novelist who wrote *Nip the Buds*, reads an article that reviews the autobiography written by the "counter-younger brother." He contacts the deformed man and agrees to serve as the consultant of the "counter-younger brother" for the first part of his autobiography, which deals with the abandonment of the fifteen boys in the village during the war. The autobiographer in a wheelchair and the consultant "talk" with each other only in writing.

The Trial experiments with the stratification of a verbal account, laminating two pairs of brothers, two different times, human consciousness and unconsciousness, today's reality and the reality of the war and the postwar period. This 1980 story, as we shall see, illustrates a new methodology that characterizes Ōe's later works: at the core of the devices of stratification is his desire to express how he is living in this reality, in this real world, how he has lived through the reality of the

1970s and 1980s, and how he has grasped these realities. Ōe relentless-
ly explores his own obsessive sense of social and historical consciousness, which he blends with lyricism and linguistic virtuosity. The
monster-like, deformed "counter-younger brother" in *The Trial* mir-
rors the multidimensional, multivocal, and polysemic worlds of a picaro, a trickster, or Günter Grass's new folk hero, the talking Flounder,
who advises his surrogate son on the male cause in different time-
phases since time immemorial. Ōe the contemporary novelist and his
marginal world of narratives inevitably project a cosmic and prophetic
vision.

3
Occupied Japan: Tales of a Gigolo

In 1934 Henry Miller wrote *Tropic of Cancer*, which became available to the American public for the first time in 1960. He wrote *Sexus* in 1949, but it was not published in the United States until 1965. Norman Mailer's *The Deer Park* appeared in 1955, "The Time of Her Time" in 1959, by which time both American novelists were already causes célèbres in Japan. An avid reader of both writers' work, Ōe published in July 1959 *Our Times* (Warera no jidai), his best-known sexually "repulsive" work, which annoyed almost all Japanese critics. It is no exaggeration to say that, without the controversial works of the two avant-garde American writers, the unfavorable reviews of *Our Times* might have driven Ōe to total despair. He was acutely aware that the "assessment of the sexual in Japanese literature is the lowest, the worst, in comparison to any other subject matter under the sun."[1] His determination to employ the sexual as the most vital methodology never diminished in the "quagmire of bad reviews." A foreign scholar of Japanese literature who was well known for her quips once said to him: "You look up words in a physiological dictionary instead of a language dictionary when you write novels, don't you?" He replied humorously, "That's correct. And I write with my genitals instead of a fountain pen!"[2]

Prior to the composition of the series of short stories that culminates in *Our Times*, Ōe admitted that he was a "writer for so-called country lads." He was resolved to break free from that label and establish himself as an "antipastoral, realistic writer."[3] To achieve this goal, he looked to the avant-garde literature of the twentieth century, whose "daring decision" is to "incorporate into the novel an unreal (*hontōra-shiku nai*) abnormality, which, it has been said, exists only in the real world, and has no business in the fictional world."[4]

With this declaration, Ōe immediately preoccupied himself with the paradox of Japan's surrender and postwar period, which means both submission and liberation at the same time. "When the nation lost a war," he once wrote about himself in the third person, "one patriotic boy in a village found that he had to cope with a gigantic seed of submission. At the same time he also began his apprenticeship, living through the postwar period with a gigantic seed of liberation and renewal."[5] What the little boy faced was the state of ambivalence: "like a watercolor . . . on which you laminate different colors before each dries up, a sense of submission, liberation, and renewal, running over and interfering with each other subtly and ambiguously, coexisting and creating a special coloration."[6] How should one outgrow (*ikino-biru*) this sense of submission without being crushed by its image, without running away from it? One must "go back to the very funda-mental roots of a consciousness of submission, or the human roots of a consciousness equipped with flesh and bones, lymphatic fluids, a stom-ach and intestinal fluids, and genitals."[7]

The choice of the sexual with its "unflagging, destructive, and shocking power" as subject also derives from his determination to surpass the postwar generation. When a Japanese literary historian talks about "postwar literature," he assumes the following four points as characteristic features of its definition: 1) it refers to those works produced during the period 1945–1952; 2) it has wedded the sexual/po-litical with literature; 3) it has strong overtones of the existentialist worldview; 4) it signals a break with the "I-novel" tradition.[8] Ōe's envy of the postwar generation was twofold: he was too young to become a postwar writer, and too young to be the contemporary reader of that generation.[9] However, he quickly realized that postwar writers had not exhausted sex and politics as new literary ingredients: "I eventually began to muster enough courage and believed that I also had the freedom to write about politics and sex, that I was free to do so."[10] The legitimization of politics/sex as a novelistic methodology, the existential outlook, and the renunciation of the confessional "I-novel" dominate the literary universe of Ōe's narratives written between 1958 and 1961.

In "Sheep" Ōe describes the relationship of XYZ that forces X (a young man) to play "sheep" twice. X is humiliated by both parties, Y (the prostitute, schoolteacher, policemen) and Z (the American soldiers as the big power). I shall now take up four narratives in which Ōe specifically experiments with variations of the XYZ relationship first introduced in "Sheep."

In "Leap Before You Look" (Miru mae ni tobe, June 1958), a twenty-year-old college student tells the story of his life with a thirty-five-year-old prostitute, Yoshie, who takes only foreigners as her customers. To follow Ōe's paradigm, the college student is X, the subjugated; Yoshie's "professional" lover, Gabriel, the subjugator, Z; and Yoshie the intermediary, Y.

The story starts with a description of the courtyard surrounded by departmental offices, where the narrator walks across the enclosure, longing for spring. "I began to feel a bitter calm getting hold of both my mind and body. It was not at all unpleasant. It simply meant that I felt a bit less cheery and youthful for a twenty-year-old" (319).[14] He continues, "But that year spring was late." This sentence implies two things: 1) spring, which gives abundant sunlight, lush leaves and the dazzling sky—the symbol of youth—does not somehow belong to him; 2) he is going to narrate to the reader a series of events that have already happened. As he crosses the courtyard at the end of winter, he sees an object, a faucet. "I realized that I was thirsty. I stopped. I had been thirsty during the entire winter" (319). He tells us that the tap water had been contaminated and the university has issued a warning that it would cause diarrhea. In other words, he knows the danger and ignores the warning.

Thus, the first page of the story already contains the basic information we have to know about the narrator. He is passive and apathetic. He first sees the object, a faucet, probably without any desire for water, because he is not looking for a faucet. He happens to see it. Then he realizes that he is thirsty. Despite the warning, he drinks the contaminated water. He could have waited to get good water somewhere else, but he does not. It is not so much urgency, we are told in his soliloquy, as indifference that drives him. He is indifferent to politics, the search for a lover, or a disease-to-come, and to reality in general. Two episodes are sufficient to illustrate his apathy, which derives from his egocentricity. First, he loathes the activists at the university, so eager to protest the Algerian War. He knows that blood is shed, but petitioning against the war does not interest him. When he has to pass by the activists, he feigns that he does not see them. He pretends that he is "a malnourished kid avoiding a bully." He refuses to sign the petition and is struck in the face by one of the activists. Even when his nose starts bleeding, he is determined more than ever not to sign the petition.

Secondly, the narrator's passive attitude and self-centered personality is revealed in his conversations with Gabriel:

> Suddenly Gabriel said, "You were saying you wanted to fight in Egypt or in Vietnam."
>
> "Oh, yeah," I said in quiet intoxication from the booze. "I want to fight. I'm sick and tired of peace. I wish that a war would break out." . . .
>
> "I've missed a lot having been born late." I yawned and stretched my back. . . .
>
> "So that's why you said you wanted to fight in Egypt or in Vietnam," Gabriel repeated. "Right?"
>
> "I will fight and sleep in the mud with the Egyptians. . . ."
>
> "When they will send me this fall to Vietnam as a foreign correspondent, there's a possibility that I may be able to take you with me."
>
> I felt strangled.
>
> "Do you intend to go?" Gabriel said coldly. He was not drunk. (325–26)

The title of the story comes from a verse which Gabriel hums after these conversations, "Look if you like, but you will have to leap." Gabriel preaches to the young college student jeeringly. "For life in general: whatever you do, you leap first before you look. There are two kinds of fellows, one who looks, the other who leaps" (326). Gabriel catches the narrator off guard, and forces him to admit his pretensions.

So far, the equilibrium in the narrator's life has been disrupted twice by his uncalled-for confrontations with Gabriel and the activist. These disequilibriums are soon brought back to the initial equilibrium: the narrator begins to forget about the humiliating experiences, and his life goes back to the former routines "with a bitter calm." At dawn Yoshie comes home and makes love to the narrator, who is half-asleep: the habitual practice of a two-year cohabitation.

Here, the story is more or less back to the starting point. The narrator is not any wiser or more enlightened after his encounters with Gabriel and the university activist, the two incidents of disequilibrium. The third disequilibrium occurs when the narrator, Yoshie, and Gabriel get drunk at a striptease joint and Gabriel starts humiliating Yoshie by descriptions of his lovemaking with her. Gabriel also reveals his contempt for Japanese: "I was a G.I. in the Korean War. A bunch of us

G.I.s once threw a little, dirty Japanese into a cesspool and drowned him. Instead of lynching us, the Japanese crowd just watched us" (330). The narrator takes his revenge on Gabriel by knocking him unconscious while he relieves himself in the dark outside. Time is a great healer for the narrator and Yoshie. They make love day and night and "by the end of summer, we forgot about the incident, an incident a bit comical and cruel."

Now, the story must start all over again. This time the narrator agrees to tutor a young woman, Yūko, who must study French to take an entrance examination for a music school. Yūko happens to be the fully clothed singer at the striptease joint, whom he once made fun of with Yoshie and Gabriel. The sexual relationship between the narrator and Yūko develops and Yūko's pregnancy—an accident—becomes the key for him to put an end to a life that is "too sterile." He abandons Yoshie in order to marry Yūko. Yūko learns that she has T.B. and must abort the baby. Abortion shatters the narrator's dream of starting a new life with Yūko. They break up; the narrator and Yoshie run into each other and the story seems to start all over again, except this time he finds himself impotent.

In "A Dark River, Heavy Oars" (Kurai kawa, omoi kai, July 1958),[15] a twelve- or thirteen-year-old junior high school boy is left behind alone while the rest of the family goes out. A prostitute lives next door and is kept by a black G.I., named Peterson. The two have a quarrel and Peterson leaves. The prostitute invites the boy to come for dinner and he gets drunk for the first time in his life. They make love. The boy falls in love with the prostitute and decides to marry her the next morning. Back in his room, the boy dozes off while he hears Peterson's return and the love-making of Peterson and the woman. On the following morning she denies knowing the boy. He realizes that he has been used as a plaything. In humiliation he has to go back to his own life, which he hates: studying to pass an entrance examination to a good high school, which in turn promises him entry to a good university with excellent employment possibilities.

The third story in which Ōe repeats the theme of a Japanese under the sway of a prostitute is called "Cheers" (Kassai, September 1958).[16] The triangular relationship of XYZ consists, respectively, of a twenty-three-year-old college student, Natsuo, a bisexual prostitute, Yasuko, and a forty-year-old French homosexual, Lucien. The narrator in "Cheers" tells us: 1) Natsuo is not hopeful for anything other than living with Yasuko; 2) he has hopes only for trivial things; 3) he has no intention of seeking a future. The intrusion of Yasuko disrupts the equilibrium of life with Lucien. Without consulting Natsuo, Lucien hires Yasuko as a short-term housekeeper. Natsuo and Yasuko make love and Natsuo realizes that he is no longer afraid of women. He decides to marry her. Lucien interferes and reveals to Natsuo that she is bisexual. Yasuko being the factor of disorientation, when she is removed Natsuo is brought back to the status quo: the humiliation of being loved by a Frenchman who despises Natsuo's fellow countrymen as dirty, yellow-skinned people. "Why am I an exception?" Natsuo feebly asks Lucien.

X, Y, and Z in the first three stories are the constants. Each story does not develop a plot, but unfolds a theme, a variation of a triangular relationship among the constants. In "Leap Before You Look," X and Y lead a more or less contented life together; in "A Dark River, Heavy Oars" it is Y and Z who live together; and in "Cheers," it is X and Z who have established a basically compatible relationship. These three sets of relationships show the three possible variations of pairs found in XYZ: X-Y, Y-Z, X-Z. How to break up the pairs is the central issue of each story. In "Leap Before You Look" the X-Y relationship is violated by the presence of Yūko. The X-Yūko pair takes over the X-Y pair. Marrying the pregnant Yūko becomes X's only hope, i.e., escape, from the status quo. In this case, the constant Z has virtually no direct impact on the X-Y relationship. "A Dark River, Heavy Oars" presents X as an element of disorientation that threatens the Y-Z pair. It is X who wants to escape from the boredom and stagnation by marrying Y. The homosexual relationship of X-Z in "Cheers" becomes strained by the appearance of Y. Heterosexuality is the key to X's freedom. X almost succeeds in escaping the cul-de-sac by marrying Y.

Our Times, the last of the series of stories that explore the image of Occupied Japan, is also Ōe's most ambitious undertaking that employs the sexual as a literary device: "I personally like this novel," Ōe wrote in an essay "Eccentricity, Abnormality, Danger in Sex," because "I do not think I will ever write another novel which is filled only with sexual words."

The fourth variation of the tripartite relationship of XYZ in this "infamous" novel concentrates again on the X-Y pair. This time, however, both Yasuo, X, and Yoriko, Y, seek a way out. Yasuo wants to start a new life by going to France. Yoriko, carrying his baby, sees him as her only escape from prostitution.[17]

The first chapter of *Our Times* describes Yasuo contemplating metaphysics in the act of lovemaking with Yoriko:

> To cogitate on metaphysics in the continual rhythmic motion of plea-sure, to preoccupy oneself with the function of spirit, this is no vulgar pastime. Slightly comical, but it is definitely stuff for grown-ups. As he soaked his elastic muscles and smooth skin in pleasure, and caressed the soft body, broken out in perspiration, of a middle-aged woman he loved, Minami Yasuo gave himself up to solitary contemplation. Solitary con-templation: but the thinking is impregnated with a sense of despair and self-abhorrence that goes in circles, a sort of desperate feeling. His lover permitted him to meditate during their lovemaking. She was a sensible and mature woman. She had enough experience to know that a young man would not be engrossed in her vagina while in embrace. She did not want it, either. So long as the young man on top of her, by contemplating something other than her body, would prolong the duration of love-making, she had nothing to complain about. So she moaned in pleasure.
>
> What one can positively call "hope" does not exist for Japanese youth. Minami Yasuo continued to cogitate with his eyes shut, knitting his eyebrows, and, in order to stabilize the position of his belly slippery from sweat, he propped himself up firmly with his elbows and knees as he extracted loud moans from the soft, hot body underneath him. (129)

Lovemaking is directly equated with the pitiful conditions into which the postwar generation is thrown. Yasuo is shackled by Yoriko, immobilized by her clinging body. His feelings are ambivalent: "It was not that he disliked to be on her body. It was simply just too hot. The sweat clung to the skin and did not evaporate" (134). Lovemaking is an indirect threat to Yasuo, because he is frightened of Yoriko's preg-nancy. He keeps saying to himself that he can find no way out, that he must escape.

A sexual act in *Our Times* means several different things. First, it is a surrender to the feminine world. To break up with Yoriko is, there-fore, a liberation from a vagina, the damp Japanese soil, human rela-tionships, and everything that is feminine. Yasuo feels that he has been "raped for an interminable time." Secondly, the repetitiousness of the act of sexual intercourse corresponds to the everyday routines in the closed world of the X-Y pair: "What you and I are going to do for the next twenty years," Yasuo says to himself, "is to shake our butts, breathe heavily, and dump five liters of sperm mixed with filth down into the dark drainage pipe. Sexual intercourse, 365 multiplied by twenty and add five for leap years, which is the number of our copula-tions. . . . Excretion, our 7,305 copulations are nothing but acts of elimination'' (145–46). Thirdly, lovemaking defines ''the sexual being'' which looks upon ''the political being'' with envy and resignation. The X-Y pair insures Yasuo the status of ''the sexual being'': ''My God, I'm a half-dead young creature, something indecent, flabby and disgusting, kept in a paradise that's cut off from everything tragic'' (137).

This sense of entrapment, a cul-de-sac, is shared by the other three characters in *Our Times*. Parallel to the main plot of the X-Y relationship runs the subplot, a story of three young men who struggle to survive as a jazz band, with a dream to lead the life of vagabonds. The trio consists of Yasuji the clarinetist, Taka the drummer, and Shigeru the pianist, who is Yasuo's younger brother.[18]

In the submission of his prize essay to the French embassy, Yasuo sees, or hopes to see, alternatives to the status quo in ''solitary confinement.'' He wins the essay contest and is awarded a scholarship for three years of study in France. He signs the contract and abandons Yoriko, who begs for a quiet life with him and the baby-to-come. He meets an Arab who persuades him to work for the Front Libération Nationale while in France. The French embassy finds this out, and Yasuo chooses not to betray the Arab friend who has offered him a sense of *solidarité*. In the end Yasuo loses everything—a chance to escape to France, Yoriko, who eventually marries one of her clients, Wilson, and Shigeru, Yasuo's only encumbrance, who chooses to commit suicide.

Yasuo is the Japanese youth who has been born too late for the heroic era. The only thing he can do is not to betray his friendship with the Arab. *Our Times* ends with his words, which echo the sentiments of the postwar generation: ''Suicide, a heroic action, is the very decisive action we can accomplish in total solitude. Suicide is the only way out of stagnation. . . . We know it, there is nothing in the world to stop us from doing it. But we continue to live, unable to muster enough courage to kill ourselves. We love, hate, make love, join in political activities, dabble in homosexuality, murder, and try to gain fame. . . . This is our times'' (302).

The narrator in ''Leap Before You Look'' concludes that he is too frightened and may never be able to make up his mind to leap. The narrator in ''Cheers'' tells us of Natsuo: ''Politics was beyond his reach. Even reality was no match for him. He was committed to absolutely nothing'' (71). In each story, X is told by Y or Z that his attempt to escape is a hopeless one, because it is not a real way out, but reexperiencing the same thing with a different partner. In "Leap Before You Look" when the narrator wants to leave Yoshie for Yūko, Yoshie retorts, "You mean your life will cease to be sterile by living with her?" (343). In "Cheers" when Natsuo tells Lucien that he has made love to Yasuko and intends to marry her, Lucien simply laughs at him, "Is that all?" Yoriko confronts Yasuo in *Our Times*: "All of a sudden, you have something to hope for? Just because you are going to France?" (252).

Throughout Ōe's four stories the protagonist, X, undergoes absolutely no change in terms of psychological development or spiritual growth.[19] In X's world, there is no reward or punishment, no trial to go through, no transgression to commit. Ōe's stories contain a potential plot, an event that could have been developed into a plot. Each protagonist of the four stories fails to make a new start, whether it is to "leap," to "gamble," or to "go abroad." The ending is inconclusive and X's philosophy ambivalent. How the X-Y pair comes to establish a relationship, or what will happen to X at the end of the story, is of little importance to Ōe.

Although Ōe has chosen in his pre-1964 works to "rewrite" four times the theme of Occupied Japan, he has not developed the theme, but has been content to describe it in variations. He has chosen only to portray the apathy, the stagnation, and the cul-de-sac of the postwar generation. As a young writer, Ōe's main concern is to identify with the problems of postwar Japanese youth, not to develop a synthesis.

4

The Image of an Embattled Cultural Hero and Picaresque Narrative

Ōe once tutored a bright junior high school student, a son of a high-ranking government official, whom he assigned to read *The Adventures of Huckleberry Finn*. The boy told Ōe curtly: "Huckleberry Finn is a real good-for-nothing [*goku tsubushi*], he doesn't accomplish anything. He cooperated with Tom Sawyer to free the black Jim, but Jim was already free in Miss Watson's will, so it was just wasted effort. Once Huckleberry Finn returns home, he immediately starts thinking about lighting out for the Territory. Doesn't he think about his future at all? He's a real good-for-nothing."[1] In the life of the bright Japanese boy there was no room for Huck Finn, and the selection of the book cost Ōe the tutorship. This particular episode, with which Ōe opens an essay, "Huckleberry Finn and the Problem of the Hero," reveals how the "good-for-nothing" hero has persisted in his imagination. Huck Finn, Ōe continues, has his descendants in Norman Mailer's Sergius O'-Shaughnessy (*The Deer Park*, 1955) and Saul Bellows' Augie March (*The Adventures of Augie March*, 1949).

Confronted with the decision "forever, betwixt two things,"[2] whether to inform on Jim or not, Huck Finn stares at the paper to be delivered to Miss Watson:

> I studied a minute, sort of holding my breath, and then says to myself:
> "All right, then, I'll go to hell"—and tore it up.
> It was awful thoughts, and awful words, but they was said. And I let

them stay said; and never thought no more about reforming. I shoved the whole thing out of my head; and said I would take up wickedness again, which was in my line, being brung up to it, and the other warn't. And for a starter, I would go to work and steal Jim out of slavery again; and if I could think up anything worse, I would do that, too; because as long as I was in, and in for good, I might as well go the whole hog.[3]

"At this point," Ōe wrote, "Huckleberry Finn has become, as it were, an existentialist hero. Mark Twain prepared a loophole for Huckleberry Finn by making Jim a freed man beforehand so that Huckleberry Finn does not have to go to hell, but he has already made that choice and plans to light out for the Territory. Beyond a doubt he will probably continue to walk the road to hell without any loopholes. He has freed himself from his time, society, and God; totally isolated . . . he has declared to himself, 'All right then, I'll go to hell.' From that moment on, he has become a hero representing America for his time and all time."[4]

Ōe concludes his discussion on the question of what is a hero: "By placing his own consciousness in the center [of his activities], a writer must span a bridge between his own terrifying solitary battle that contains an individual death, and the entire world in which countless numbers of people come and go. The face of one human being links individuals, society, and the world, and thus he plays a basic and ultimate function. So this is how a writer sets out in search of a hero."[5] Whether a hero dies by bullets like John F. Kennedy, or turns antisocial like Charles A. Lindbergh, or simply considers living on a raft completely at freedom his best life, what is our hero like, Ōe seems to be saying, who represents Japan since the end of the Second World War? Or, do we have a hero?

In his pre-1964 narratives Ōe continuously explores the image of an "embattled cultural hero,"[6] a descendant of Huck Finn. At the same time he portrays again and again the counter-image of this hero, whom he often models after himself as a writer. This antihero, for example, frequently appears as a college student who, in his attempt to commit himself to sociopolitical causes or to make a new start in his uneventful, disenchanted life, tastes the bitter reality of a contemporary society filled with deception, violence, and corruption. While Ōe's hero goes against the grain, undergoes sexual/criminal adventures, and lives a short, fast life, the antihero is a real survivor, whom Ōe often assigns the role of raconteur to relate the life of the hero. The assessment Ōe makes of these two types of young man suggests that both these youths, the hero and the antihero, ultimately embody marginality and ambiguity, positioning themselves on the periphery of society.

A Western literary type that comes closest to Ōe's ambiguous, marginal characters is the Spanish-born picaro. The comparison is not a far-fetched one, since Huck Finn and Augie March, who captivated Ōe's mind, have been regarded by critics as picaresque heroes.[7] The picaro is a "rogue," both a hero and an antihero, who lives by his wits; an orphaned vagabond forced by circumstances to go "on the road," who tells of his life and adventures in an episodic fashion. In the narrow sense of the word, Ōe's narratives do not belong to the "picaresque" genre. However, reading his works involves what we might call the picaresque experience, which is "an exercise of mind, really a reveling in the mind as a conqueror, a relishing of power through purely mental rather than physical or political or social means."[8] It is due to this peculiar aesthetic vantage point that we can explain why Ōe's reader is freed from moral concern or emotional trials even in the midst of the violent physical ordeals the young protagonists undergo. In the following discussion of the image of the embattled cultural hero and the antihero, I would like to draw upon the concept of picaresque narrative as a point of reference and comparison.

The Youth Who Came in Late (Okurete kita seinen, 1962, hereafter *The Youth*) provides an early example of how Ōe attempts to create an existentialist hero through a picaro-like character. The narrator/protagonist of the novel shares with Ōe the experience of Japan's defeat in the war as a young boy. His life story stands as a testimony of how difficult it is to "decide, forever, betwixt two things" and continue to "walk the road to hell" in contemporary society. Calling his "memoir" an "apology of a lonely soldier in a dubious battle" (257),[9] the narrator opens with the description of his boyhood in a village on Shikoku. As an eleven-year-old boy, his rebellious spirit matches that of Huck Finn, as he refuses to accept the chicanery, deception, and manipulation of the adults' world. There is a fundamental difference, however, between the worlds of the two boys. For Ōe's young character, the children's world is as cruel as that of adults.

One instance of this cruelty is the narrator's first English lesson, conducted by the head teacher, nicknamed Hare. He was a "recruiter" who sent the young men in the village to the volunteer army. His immediate obsession with letting his hair grow only started on the day following the Emperor's "broadcast" that announced the termination of the war, and revealed to the Japanese for the first time the human voice of their divine Emperor. The enemy language, English, is now the most welcomed language in Japan, and Hare summons the elementary school children to the playground:

> "Now, everybody together, say haroh" the passionate man on the podium shouted.
>
> The children burst into laughter and fell silent, and did not shout back haroh. On the podium Hare gave an awkward grin, tightened the facial muscles that formed into a lonely insidious look. . . .
>
> "Now, everybody together, haroh!"
>
> "Haroh!" a few voices followed suit.
>
> "Now, louder, try again, haroh, haroh!"
>
> "Haroh! Haroh! Ooooooooooo!" the majority went along.
>
> . . .
>
> The first batch to shout back were the children of the evacuees. Their cheeks flushed with the summer heat, shame, and excitement, their eyes moist, they shouted back with aggressive force. I kept silent, but my tiny silence, the tiny silence of a child, was on a minuscule scale. I was merely a strand of seaweed adrift on the ocean of a big chorus of haroh's. I did not exist. All of a sudden, I felt I was being pulverized and gulped down into a hole. And anxiety ripened.
>
> "Haroh means, 'Mighty glad to see you' in Japanese, you say to a guest, Mighty glad to see you, Mighty glad to see you, Haroh, Haroh! Come on!"
>
> "Haroh, haroh, haroh! Mighty glad to see you, Mighty glad to see you, Mighty glaaaaad to seeeeehh yoooooooouuu!"
>
> "Amida Buddha, Amida Buddha!" I heard the words forced out of my throat.
>
> "Haroh, haroh, haroh!"
>
> "Amida Buddha, Amida Buddha!"
>
> Someone's fist struck the back of my head. I turned around and saw an upperclassman, an evacuee, standing. . . . Anger blinded my eyes. . . .
>
> "Shameless country bumpkin," the evacuee student said in a loud voice so that his friends could hear it. "He said, Amida Buddha, what a dingbat, Amida buddha, that country bumpkin." (67–68)

Betrayed by the children, the young boy is totally alone. Comradeship is denied him except for the brief moments he shares with Kō, a Korean boy, an outsider in the village. Outrage, frustration, and despair overtake him as he sees the world disintegrate right before his eyes.

The boy witnesses a similar betrayal acted out by the adults: Japanese selling out their own countryman to the Occupation Army when a crime is committed by the "enemy." After the arrival of the Occupation troops, one of the soldiers rapes the eighteen-year-old shamaness of the *Takajoshu* (the aborigines of Shikoku Island). Seeking to avenge her, a young *Takajo* man stabs the G.I. and goes into hiding in the forest with the girl. The entire village agrees to conduct a manhunt when the interpreter of the American troop, "a foreigner who speaks Japanese," demands that they hand over the assailant.

> Right beside me was the owner of the drugstore standing with his arms folded as he watched the [village] representatives walk over to the jeep.
>
> "Are they really going to catch the criminal and hand him over?" I asked him.
>
> "Yup. Sure, they mean business," the owner of the drugstore said curtly as he shot a glance at me.
>
> "But we hand a Japanese over to the enemy?"
>
> "The enemy? You damn fool! The Occupation Army is no enemy of ours, and how can the *Takajoshu* be Japanese?"
>
> I did not understand him, even if I wanted to, I felt I would not be able to understand him. From that moment on, even though he was sweating like me in the same scorching air, I felt that he was a disgusting, yellow, squishy caterpillar, entirely different from me. Riled and irritated, I spat. My kid brother followed suit and spat in a circle.
>
> "Why are the *Takajoshu* Japanese like us, why are they our ally!" the owner of the drugstore was mumbling to himself repeatedly as if in a hot temper. (74–75)

As Ōe introduces a marginal character, Kō, who plays the special role of "dissenter" among the children, he brings the narrator and an adult "dissenter" together to be united briefly over the rescue operation of the shamaness and the *Takajo* man hiding in the forest. One of the three "conscientious objectors" in the village selects the narrator to carry out a dangerous mission: outpace the manhunt, locate the pair in hiding, and deliver money for their escape. The boy continues all night long in the depths of the formidable forest until he spots two black, swaying shadows hanging from a tree. This incident reinforces in the boy's mind a sense of total uselessness and isolation: "I'm not even needed by these corpses. I've been born late, real trash . . ." (98).

The children's world and the adults' world comfortably merge, and the denizens of the former quickly learn the convenience of "revising history" and the art of lying from the police chief in regard to the disappearance of the *Takajoshu*, whose settlement has been burned down:

> "The *Takajo* settlement has never existed in this village, there's been no *Takajo* god, the *Takajoshu* never existed. If an outsider asks you, tell him you don't know anything about them, you've never heard of them! Got that? Those who understand me, raise your hands! Scholars have written, college professors have written, that the Shikoku aborigines were annihilated several thousand years ago. Books don't make mistakes. If you spread lies about the *Takajoshu*, I'll put you in prison. Now they say we've got a democratic society, but I'm no democrat. Got that? Raise your hands!" (99)

During the short period of time between the announcement of the termination of the war by the "human" Emperor and the "arrest" of the young boy by police who send him to a reform school, Ōe packs in incident after incident to inform the reader of how the world, especially the adult world, corners, betrays, and abandons the young "patriotic" boy. It is as if Ōe were preparing and educating him to become a picaro, a protean figure who knows the art of deceit and deception, whose immediate concern is to alleviate the emptiness of a belly or pocket. Survival is his art.[10]

In this spirit of picaresque narrative, Ōe lets the young boy, now a grown-up, again speak about his own life and adventures in the second part of *The Youth*. How does an ex-reform school child cope with the postwar environment in a metropolis, Tokyo? How does he apply the knowledge acquired from his experience of the manipulations of the adults? Now a political science major at Tokyo University, the narrator recounts a series of farcical events that befall him, all originating from the 200,000 yen he agrees to procure for Ikuko, his French-language pupil, from her father, a powerful conservative politician, Sawada Toyohiko. This man's daughter, who needs the money to have an abortion, asks the narrator for another favor: to persuade her sixteen-year-old "lover" to allow the operation. Why does the narrator get himself involved with jobs of such a delicate nature, knowing he will fail? His reasoning is as simple and commonsensical as that of a picaro, a half-outcast "loner," a trickster, and an amusing vagabond. Once he has set out to pursue the cult of success, the narrator's first step is to ingratiate himself with a powerful "master." Sawada Toyohiko is the most ideal choice for the young social climber.

Like the picaro, the narrator is an "outsider who wants to get in."[11] He repeats this pattern of moving "from exclusion to attempted inclusion and back to exclusion"[12] with political radicals. When Sawada shows no interest in lending him 200,000 yen, the narrator turns to his leftist friend, Kitada, to secure a cheap doctor for Ikuko's abortion. In return for this favor, Kitada asks him to join "The Society of Japan in Struggle" as his substitute while he fights in Nasser's army in Egypt.

In his farcical entanglement with the radical organization, the narrator is mistaken for a "spy" and suffers "a most shameful torture" at the hands of his leftist friends. The entire fiasco reveals the narrator's opportunism, gullibility, and incapability of feeling any deep emotions except hatred. The reader is not quite certain why, aside from pride and a sense of embarrassment, the narrator does not try to save his own skin. We are left to assume that, since "part of the human condition is to hurt and be hurt,"[13] the narrator's incarceration as a spy suspect, which was brought on him by his own free will, means it is his turn to be hurt. Ōe refuses to let the reader feel the real pain experienced by the narrator during the "interrogation." Here the effect of the narrative is similar to that intended by Cervantes or Rabelais in their works. Ōe expects us to "be amused by the spectacle of very real pain" and seems to remind us of the picaresque situation that, if the innocent victim of a crude practical joke suffers, he has only gotten what a person who has let himself be tricked deserves.[14]

What we see throughout *The Youth* is the narrator standing somewhere between the worlds of a criminal and a picaro, or, between the respectable world and the criminal world. A by-product of the war, an ex-reform school child, a heroin addict, and a sexually impotent social climber, the narrator's personality is that of a psychopath. When everything he does backfires, the narrator, exhausted and at his wits' end, lets the politician Sawada have his way: ". . . at a nice, quiet place, wait for a time of your own. You're already one of the contemporary elites" (339). The young man "in a dubious battle" ends the memoir with his pronouncement that he is going to be a homosexual and sadly notes: "I am neither a hero who would stir up man's passions nor a witness to any era. I am just like you" (343).

This blundering antihero seems to echo the Sartrean view that "what all people want, some without being aware of it, is to be witness to their time, their lives and, above all, themselves."[15] Ōe describes in *Outcries* (Sakebigoe, 1962) an existentialist hero who passionately tries to be witness to his time in the most negative way, by committing a murder. He carries out this most outrageous crime against an individual and society in order to stake out a land of his own, a world of his own where he can live "authentically." Ōe's interest, however, does not lie in the description of a crime per se, but in the relationship of marginal types who surround the criminal-to-be, and in the sociopolitical implications of the criminal act. A twenty-year-old student again plays the role of a narrator, an antihero whose life has offered no tragedies, no accidents, no love lost, no feeling except the fear of V.D.: "That nothing ever happened to me was the only characteristic of my first twenty years of life" (11).[16] He neither joins nor rejects society; he is simply gripped with a desire to get out of Japan.

The narrator, a marginal by choice, comes in contact with two other young men who are marginals by circumstances. Tiger and Takao represent two racially oppressed groups in Japan: blacks and Koreans. Their mixed ethnic origins automatically provide them with the status of outcasts, "unauthentic" residents in Japan. Tiger, a seventeen-year-old, who has been brought up in an orphanage, says to the narrator: "They say there's no racial discrimination in Japan. That's what the people at orphanages believe, but I know that's not true. I know how racism comes out"(18). Likewise, Takao, one year older than Tiger, has been brought up in a slum by his Japanese mother, who throughout his childhood constantly warns her son that he should never reveal his real identity, and then sends him out to live among Japanese as a Japanese.

These three youths are brought together by another marginal, a young homosexual American, Darius Serbezov, who has developed a relapse of epilepsy after a traumatic experience in the Korean War. He plans a European trip on a yacht, the *Les Amis*, which is under construction. A harmonious world filled with affection, comradeship, and anticipation disintegrates when Darius is charged with molesting a retarded boy and deported to America. Every fund-raising campaign for the *Les Amis* fails. In desperation Tiger decides to rob a bank. He takes Takao to the Yokosuka Base to "rehearse" a robbery with a toy machine gun, is shot by the M.P.s, and dies.

The story of *Outcries* then focuses on the Korean boy, Takao, who is totally isolated after he has a fight with the narrator over Tiger's death. Ōe brings in an omniscient narrator who describes the transformation Takao undergoes from a discontented, apolitical being to a political being, from an "unauthentic" person to an "authentic" person in a world of "monsters." The main problem this criminal hero has to face is how he can prove the authenticity of his own experience: "I am rejected by this real world. I am not an authentic human being here. I have indirectly established that I am a monster from a country of my own making. Even though I always felt this world had rejected me as a bastard child, I still fought hard to get in and savor the security of being a legitimate child. But it was all wrong. All wrong. Before I realized it, I had set off on a Japanese ship to get out, built up my hopes on a plan to go on a trip abroad, etc. Of course, everything failed . . . ''(99).

On the day before the crime takes place, Takao is "not even a sex criminal, or a cowardly, vulgar Peeping Tom" (93). As the smallest, most insignificant monster in the universe, all he can do is to fantasize sexual crimes. At night, out of frustration, he throws a stone into the crowded residential area. When it fails to hit anything, he concludes: "Even when I throw a stone, nothing happens. It is as if I didn't exist in this world" (94).

After he strangles a high school girl, Takao becomes an unusual criminal. He wants the whole world to know he has committed a murder. He starts his "self-advertisement" in order to "maintain the monster-ness" by calling a newspaper company: "Me? I am a monster" (97). He manipulates the mass media. However, his happiness in being a monster is short-lived, because impersonators and fakes begin to compete with him to destroy his authenticity as the "true" monster: "He became an unhappy monster" (101). To secure the authentic life of a monster, he turns himself in, and at his first trial he is sentenced to death. At the court when his mother calls him Ochan, a name he has never heard before, he immediately realizes that it is his real Korean name: "Ochan. . . . At that moment Kure Takao thought he was given a clue as to why he had become a bastard child in this world, why he had not been able to possess the sense of security, of living with authenticity in this world. From the time when his mother forced him to live as the fake Japanese Kure Takao, instead of the Korean Ochan, he began to lose the sense of being a legitimate child" (104).

For an existentialist hero like Takao, to live authentically is to "be aware of his freedom and responsibility of choice—above all of the original choice of his life."[17] However, from the beginning of his life, Takao has been denied freedom and responsibility of choice by his own mother and society. His Korean father, a hermit, who has finally been located in the wilderness of Hokkaido after his son's death sentence, comments sarcastically on the core of the problem: "My son has been brought up neither as a Korean nor a Japanese; just a nobobdy. So he probably wanted to become at least a criminal!" (102). Takao's criminal act marks the most "original choice of his life," which he must carry out of his own free will, and of which society must take notice. As an exile in a strange land, he finds the world to be "gratuitous and absurd'' and totally unresponsive; like the Sartrean hero, he passionately tries to seek the "meaning of man's separation from himself and from the world.''[18] By doing so, he condemns himself and is condemned by the world.

Based on an actual murder committed by a Korean boy on September 1, 1958 (commonly called the "Komatsugawa Case"),[19] *Outcries* seems to be a result of Ōe's efforts to "create a literature of extreme situations''[20] that focuses on the "isolation of the existing individual.'' However, the solitary responsibility of the individual does not come to an end with the death sentence of Takao, and Ōe brings back into the story as narrator the young college student, who has neither made the original choice of his life nor discovered what it is to do such a thing. He witnesses the embattled cultural hero being transformed from a monster into a gentle creature, totally reconciled to himself and ready to die: "Kure Takao was too quiet, pleasant, and generous,'' the narrator tells us. When he reluctantly breaks the news of the letter of invitation written in Paris by Darius, who does not know anything about Tiger and Takao, the young prisoner reminisces about Tiger: "Tiger was the one who should have set off with the ticket Darius Serbezov is going to send. We should have given him a chance to hop around on African soil. Tiger really wanted to take off, and knew his destination. And how young he was'' (109).

In the end, left behind by Tiger and Takao, both of whom had found a land of their own, the narrator leaves for Europe, which turns out to offer him nothing more than the life of a fugitive: "Once I set out on the journey, I began to feel I wanted to put off my reunion with Darius Serbezov as long as possible. It was something like being put on probation. . . . I felt that I was throwing off a gigantic responsibility, abandoning a heavy load on the ground; I fancied that I was avoiding and escaping from it'' (113). There is no place for him, where he can live comfortably; the narrator abruptly ends his story with cries of terror echoing in his ears as Darius Serbezov tries patiently to woo him.

This ambiguous relationship between a hero and an antihero is taken up again in *Adventures of Everyday Life* (Nichijōseikatsu no bōken, 1964, hereafter *Everyday Life*), in which "I,'' a young writer, relates the life and adventures of a "rogue'' (*akkan*), Saiki Saikichi. This picaresque hero lures both the writer and the reader into his world of tricks and ultimately becomes a symbol for the artist. Instead of combining the elements of artist and picaro in one character as Thomas Mann did with Felix Krull, Ōe plays off the world of a young artist against that of a picaresque hero, implying that the "hero's rascalities are a vivid comic symbol for all the 'oddities' that accompany talent."[21] According to the narrator, somewhere between the two choices of being either "an adventurous washout (*dekizokonai*) hero" or an "antihero who has given up setting out and sits still at home" lies the artist's professional *modus vivendi*, "his skill, ingenuity, working with head rather than body, with individual artifice rather than group planning."[22] Saiki Saikichi's "rascalities" prove to be the *sine qua non* for the emotional, intellectual life of the novice writer.

From the very beginning of the novel, it is the narrator's objective to try to lure the reader into his world, at the center of which is the memory of Saikichi, and to take us into his confidence. He establishes the intimate writer-reader relationship by directly addressing us:

> Have you imagined the pain you suffer when you receive a letter which says that a friend of yours committed suicide for unknown reasons at a strange, far away place like a republic on Mars, a friend with whom you had lots of fights, but who had been on your mind for a long time? . . . I have just received a letter via Paris which informed me that in a city called Bougie in a North African country which has just won independence, a dear friend of mine, Saiki Saikichi, hanged himself with a belt that he let dangle from the shower faucet in a bathroom at a hotel. (129)[23]

Throughout his biographical tale of the rogue, the narrator makes sure that the reader has not misunderstood him: "I felt Saikichi was calling out to me, crying out in terror. I was in communion with him. In fact, he was in pain all that time. Please do not think that I have something of the mystic in me" (275). At another time he wants to test our faithfulness as readers: "Do you still remember his [Saikichi's] words about another species of *homo sapiens* with a different physical make-up?" (182). Or, he is sometimes apologetic about his desultory narration: "Probably it is too capricious for me to break up the sequential order of the story, but there is no neat order in the world of memories" (149). But more than anything else, his ego matters to him; our reactions to his hero are of the utmost importance to him: "I am afraid of the harsh treatment my hero might receive from you at this stage in the narrative, by what one might call contemptuous indifference" (150). Furthermore, as in picaresque narrative, we become aware of the double perspective of the "narrating or remembering 'I'" who is the young writer and the "remembered 'he'" who is the rascal: "The *act* of telling is itself a 'trick,' a lure, the fictional analogy of the tricks of which the picaro's life and the world are composed."[24] Saikichi's rascalities seem to embody the paradox that the "artist is only a picaro," or, conversely, "the picaro is really an artist."[25]

Since garrulity was one of Saikichi's characteristics, the narrator admits that, unfortunately, he has to summarize some of the adventures his hero recounted to him. Among his many unique characteristics, Saikichi was an "inveterate betrayer," a "pathological liar," a "car thief," and a "good impersonator." He was also irresponsible, aloof, "indifferent to suffering—his own and that which he caused,"[26] and had a taste for the "high life." Even in his final performance, in death, no one can be sure that the picaro is not merely somehow using artifice. Saikichi's first wife sends the narrator a postcard which says, "Wasn't his death a trick?" (378). As the enumeration of Saikichi's characteristics continues, we become deeply steeped in the world of the picaro.

In comparison to this adventurous world, either actually experienced by or recounted to the narrator, the biography of the young novice writer, which moves in parallel to Saikichi's story, is totally boring, insignificant, and inconsequential. Saikichi is his only friend, his only point of contact with other beings. Saikichi is a raconteur, the young writer a listener: "Since I have been attacked by hypochondria, I have been terribly lonely. I felt that having such a friend who would talk to me continuously was invaluable. All I had to do was to keep my mouth shut, since I had nothing to talk about. I wanted to be spoken to incessantly. Saiki Saikichi was the angel who made the golden dream of a hypochondriac come true" (178).

Apart from writing a "requiem" for a dear friend, what is it that the narrator wants to tell us of this "unusual young man among those who were born between 1935 and 1940," who meditated on the fundamental questions of morality, sexual desire, courage, sincerity, mercy, and the meaning of life? "I want to write about his virtues, with an urgency that cries out . . . that Saiki Saikichi was an adventurer. . . . With his coaching I was able to experience all kinds of adventures on the track of everyday life" (132). Despite their differences, the narrator tells us that he has learned from Saikichi.

However, since his "coach" is a "rogue," what the narrator actually undergoes with Saikichi often amounts to helping him out financially, delivering him out of an awkward situation, or simply being forced by circumstances to play the role of a voyeur. The rest of the "adventures" involve intellectual exercises on various subjects ranging from drama, morality, and lovemaking techniques to the fate of *homo sapiens*. For example, when Saikichi relates the experience of sleeping with a forty-year-old nymphomaniac and a boy, the narrator readily admits: "I am embarrassed to tell you this, but the idea of Saikichi's *mènage à trois* with the boy and the corpulent woman did excite me" (163). He later sees Saikichi in action with his first wife, Himiko, both of whom have stayed overnight at the narrator's apartment: "Around noon when I got up to urinate, Mr. and Mrs. Saiki Saikichi were making love on the sofa in my study like contented animals in a rear entry position which Saikichi, a master hand at sex, decided is the most rewarding position. In coitus, Saikichi and Himiko turned their heads slowly around and looked at me, as if seeing indifferently a stranger passing through in the distance. . . . I felt like a Peeping Tom" (185–86).

Besides functioning as a coach, Saikichi provides materials for the young writer's books: "When you want to describe a sexual pervert, my stories will be useful to you" (157). He also criticizes the finished product: "I read two of your stories. Your style is as ponderous as a medieval knight's armor!" (165).

By describing the biography of this antiromantic, antipastoral hero, Ōe playfully parodies the Japanese "I-novel" subgenre. According to this tradition, the author must candidly and sincerely recount in the worst possible light his own private world, which is supposedly filled with anguish, self-doubt, and self-deception. With this highly personal and confessional quality, the "I-novel" requires that "literature be 'truthful,' " meaning "accuracy in recording: . . . honesty in disclosure! . . . sincerity in confession."[27] It is important to note here that *Everyday Life* is the only novel Ōe has written in which he makes use of his autobiography between 1956 and 1963. One could say that, in the absence of the Saikichi narrative, the young writer's life is identical to Ōe's. Ōe is honestly and truthfully recording his own life in the manner of the "I-novel." However, the life of the rascal is his own invention. Here Ōe is parodying traditional autobiographical fiction which abandons art and fictionality and instead takes refuge in convention.

After their first encounter at a meeting of volunteer soldiers for the Suez War, the twenty-one-year-old narrator takes Saikichi, three years his junior, to his birthplace, a village on Shikoku, to solicit funds from his grandfather for the sea voyage to Egypt. Saikichi succeeds in charming the old man, receives the money, and leaves the unfortunate narrator behind with a case of measles. For the next two years, there is no word from Saikichi.

The narrator in the meantime publishes a short story about a student's part-time job of killing dogs ("A Strange Job," 1957) and begins to make some money writing for magazines. He happens to see Saikichi in a film advertisement in a magazine and looks him up. Saikichi tells him of his "exodus" on a treasure-hunt ship. Saikichi disappears again, and another two years pass, during which the narrator has "started a writing career. I moved into a bigger apartment and wrote every day. I received one award [the Akutagawa Prize for "Prize Stock," 1958] and published books. . . . I joined the writers' delegation to the People's Republic of China and met Mao Zedong [June 1960]" (170). While Saikichi is absent, the young writer struggles hard to establish his career. Prior to the reappearance of his picaro, the narrator experiences blackmail for the first time: "A cruel, political story I wrote a few months before helped mushrooms of anger proliferate inside the heads of all kinds of people ["A Political Boy Is Now Dead," 1961].[28] Day and night thorny squalls of threatening phone calls and letters began to pour in on me. I felt so isolated, developed a kind of hypochondria, and no longer wrote stories or essays. I ate six times a day, chewed on antacid tablets, rode around on a bike, did some body-building with an expander and dumbbells, and avoided anything intellectual" (171).

This writer's slump is almost a death to the narrator. But Saikichi helps him start an "anti-ivory tower" life (*hanshosai seikatsu*). The narrator postpones his wedding indefinitely and withdraws all his savings to buy a used car to go in search of some adventure: "Saiki Saikichi came back to rescue me out of hypochondria, to invite me to the adventures of everyday life, with a tiny, rebellious wife, who looked like his sister" (172). Under the guidance of Saikichi, the narrator encounters marginal types with whom he slowly widens his experiential horizon: Himiko, who calls herself one of the great women in Henry Miller's "The Land of Fuck"; a young Korean boxer, Kimtai, who leads a short but glorious life as a bantamweight champion; a young A-bomb victim, Akatsuki, who suffers from leukemia; Saikichi's second wife, Takako, who provides her young husband with "a gorgeous, luxurious life."

The end of the anti-ivory tower life also marks the end of the intimacy between the coach and the trainee. The narrator decides "to swim back to the shore of a writing career" (309) and defends his change of heart: "If there is someone who admonishes me for not being able to become a faithful pupil of that adventurer of everyday life, called Saikichi, I intend to accept it silently" (311).

Everyday Life, the tale of a rascal, means many different things to the narrator: it is a "requiem," a song for the evocation of Saikichi's soul, and for the repose of the artist's own desolate soul. It is also a portrait of a hero who is "one of my contemporaries, a man of my time" (377). And this picaro-figure is a reflection of the writer's profession that revels in the mind as conqueror in search of a hero, and of what Ōe calls "literary adventures." When the narrator ends the biography saying, "If he wrote me now from the Sahara Desert, I would leave everything behind and join him" (378), so is the reader ready to follow the narrator and resume any sort of adventures with Saikichi.

*   *   *

In Ōe's narratives that deal with the adventures of the rogue, the criminal, or the antihero, there is, ultimately, ambiguity. With the heroic and the contemporary placed in an ambiguous juxtaposition, whether by circumstances or by choice, the young protagonists must occupy the "truly marginal position of being a 'half-outsider' who can neither reject nor join his fellow men."[29] Comradeship denied them, Ōe's isolated young individuals are misfits who look at man and the world from the margins of society. However, because of their marginality, they are also capable of sharp satiric observation of society as they hold the middle position between the respectable world and the criminal world.[30] And, as is the case with picaresque narrative, Ōe's marginal world is "to be continued," for his antihero's lot in life is to survive and outgrow the isolation of the "merely" existing individual, seemingly trapped in this world. It is inevitable that this antihero type, the embattled cultural hero, is to continue his adventures in Ōe's post-1964 narratives, reemerging as a young father who challenges society and the world with his idiot son.

5

A Narrative of Simultaneity: *The Football Game of the First Year of Manen*

The 1967 award-winning novel, *The Football Game of the First Year of Manen* (Manengannen no futtobōru, hereafter *Manen*), tells of the adventures of two brothers who return to their native village in the valley on Shikoku, in search of their roots and to start a new life. As this story, set in 1960, moves toward the future, there is another story that moves back into the past, the tale of the two brothers' great-grandfather and his younger brother, who were involved in the Manengannen (1860) uprising. And crosscutting the development of the two stories is the private quest of the narrator, Mitsusaburo: to seek the meaning of his only friend's death. *Manen* is Ōe's first post-1964 novel that experiments with "multilayeredness" and simultaneity of narrative discourse. A reading of *Manen* requires more than tracking the "unfolding of the story": it requires us "to recognize in it a number of 'strata,' to project the horizontal concatenations of the narrative onto an implicitly vertical axis; to read a narrative . . . is not only to pass from one word to the next, but also from one level to the next."[1]

What holds the horizontal concatenations of the narrative onto an implicitly vertical axis, Ōe explains in "The Football of Simultaneity," is a kind of clamp: "To be straightforward, isn't the writer's imagination something like a clamp that holds two different dimensions together? . . . These two different dimensions function as an effective, basic unit when we discuss a novel. Many sets of this unit place themselves on top of one another in layers, giving a unique and complex shape to the novel. The clamp which holds together each basic unit of the two different dimensions is the very imagination of the writer, which is also his flesh. Since this clamp is also flesh and blood, it is neither hard nor stable like an iron clamp. The very nature of the clamp is its soft, dangerous, and unstable dynamism.''[2]

Manen is Ōe's attempt to drive his own imaginative clamp into two different historical periods: the first year of Manen, 1860, and his own time, 1960. The purpose of this clamp, he continues, is to "reveal the simultaneity that helps two different time periods communicate with each other dynamically. I tried to have the first year of Manen and 1960 confront each other with the dark void of one hundred years between them. The ball kicked by the people in the first year of Manen bounces over the one-hundred-year abyss, and hits the people in 1960. The same ball kicked back by the people in 1960 takes flight again back toward the first year of Manen.''[3] Of course, the ball Ōe is talking about is neither a soccer ball nor a rugby ball, but a football representing one of the important objects of contemporary American culture. This is no accident because both years, 1860 and 1960, mark major historical/political events that brought Japan and the United States closer together. In 1860 the Tokugawa government, forced to open up to the West by the arrival of Commodore Perry and his "black ship," sent an embassy to the United States to obtain ratification of the commercial treaty that had been signed two years earlier. In 1960 the Japanese government signed the renewal of the Japan–United States Security Treaty (commonly called Ampo). The period 1959–1960 proved to be one of the most tumultuous in recent history, in which the government and the main leftist student organization, Zengakuren, clashed repeatedly over Ampo.

Although Ōe does not deal with these two turbulent historical events directly, they distinctly reverberate in the background throughout the novel, providing its historical/political framework. For example, Ōe throws in the story of John Manjiro (Nakahama Manjiro, 1827–1898), whom the narrator's great-grandfather once met. A shipwrecked fisherman, Manjiro was picked up by an American ship and taken to the United States where, for ten years, he received an American education. In 1851 he returned to Japan, which was in the midst of a political upheaval toward the end of Tokugawa rule. Between 1851 and 1898 his knowledge of navigation and the English language was crucial for the Tokugawa government and the subsequent Meiji government in dealing with the United States.

John Manjiro is the epitome of the adventurous spirit for Takashi, Mitsusaburo's younger brother, as well as for his great-grandfather's younger brother. Ōe casually mentions in the first chapter that Takashi was a political activist who participated in the violent Ampo demonstrations of June 1960. Also caught up in this political incident is the narrator's "only friend," who eventually committed suicide: in front of the Diet Building, to protect his newlywed wife from the onslaught of the riot squad, "he had his head bashed in by a police riot-stick" (19/13).[4] He became a manic-depressive, and in the end "stripped himself, painted his entire head vermilion, thrust a cucumber up his anus and hanged himself" (9/4).

Later in the tale, the narrator imagines a fusion of 1860 and 1960, of his brother Takashi and his great-grandfather's brother, the coexistence of synchronic and diachronic time:

> The snow had not let up. A strange *idee fixe* was born inside me: the idea that I could capture and maintain all the lines traced by the snow-flakes in one second as they continued to fall through the space of the valley, that there was no other movement of the snow. The essence of one second expanded to infinity. The sounds sucked in by the film of snow, the orientation of time was also engulfed and vanished in the falling snow. A ubiquitous "time." Running naked, Takashi was the great-grandfather's younger brother and my own brother. In this one split second were all the moments of one hundred years packed tightly together in strata. (144/146)

The two brothers' attempts to come to grips with their past—their only mutual obsession—each approaching it with completely antithetical methods, become the very rhythm of the text of *Manen*. The narrative is constructed on the principle of thesis and antithesis: Takao's version of what happened to his great-grandfather's younger brother in the Manengannen uprising, and Mitsusaburo's refutation of it. The six rounds of the "debate" between the two brothers determine the to-and-fro movement of the narrative discourse. Each round of the match prods Mitsusaburo into divulging more information about the uprising, which he has either remembered reading about or hearing about from his mother.

As we learn more about the uprising, the narrator at the same time exposes the reader to the intimate portrait of the troubled youth, Takashi. His psychopathic behavior also follows pendular motion: from violence to penitence back to violence. As a result, the reader must be aware of three movements going back and forth simultaneously: the metaphoric "football" being tossed back and forth between 1860 and 1960; the seesaw verbal game, "Did the younger brother of the great-grandfather become a turncoat after the Manengannen uprising or didn't he?"; Takashi's unstable and dangerous personality leading alternately to acts of penitence and violence.

Takashi's objective in life is to relive the violent world of his great-grandfather's younger brother. As an organizer of the football team for the young men of the village, and a leader of the "riot of imagination" that enables the young men to leap back "one hundred years to feel the thrill of recreating the Manengannen uprising," Takashi comments on the relationship between violence and mankind: "Cadavers and madness are the most unadulterated signs of violence. . . . When I think about violence, I'm baffled by the fact that my own ancestors who stood up against violence were able to outgrow it and even succeeded in begetting me. They lived through a time of terrifying violence. When I think of the amount of violence those people connected with me had to stand up against, it makes me dizzy" (141/143).

The sense of dizziness the reader experiences, however, does not come so much from the amount or the nature of the violence described in *Manen* as from the pendulum motion of violence-penitence-violence that characterizes Takashi's fast, short life. All the violence he commits is designed to create the atmosphere of an uprising that would give him a chance to play the role of the sacrificial lamb. As a teenager he raped his retarded little sister. He tries to make up for this act through participation in the collective action of the Ampo demonstrations. He then joins a drama troupe made up of "converted" Ampo activists who tour the United States with a play called "Our Shame." He teaches his young "bodyguards," Hoshio and Momoko, that they "must live sober." Once back in his native village, he organizes a riot and leads in the looting of a supermarket owned by a Korean nicknamed "The Emperor." To whip up the carnivalesque spirit that allows everyone to take part in the looting as equals, Takashi revives an old village festival, the Nenbutsu Dance. He beats up one of the football team members who has tried to seduce Momoko. He commits "incest" with Natsumi, the alcoholic and sexually troubled wife of Mitsusaburo. He then tells his brother that he has raped a girl and bashed her head in with a rock. Takashi tries to perform his final penitence by offering his eyes to Mitsusaburo, whose right eye is without vision.

In a final confrontation Ōe builds up the dialectic tension between the two brothers by casting Mitsusaburo in the dual role of prosecutor/

defense attorney, with Takashi the defendant who wants to be lynched by the villagers. Although Mitsusaburo accuses Takashi for his violent acts and the lie about the brutal murder and rape of the girl, Mitsusaburo simultaneously defends his brother, claiming he is innocent:

> Since Takashi backed away from us [Mitsusaburo and Hoshio], drawing the gun close to his body with a snappiness which was out of joint with his sluggish air, Takashi and I stood face to face with an appropriate distance between us for a debate.
>
> "Taka, I hear you tried to rape the girl and smashed her head in with a rock when she put up a fight, but that's not what happened, is it?" I blasted off my accusation.
>
> "Ask Gii the hermit, get him to tell you what he saw!" Takashi immediately and violently rebutted in a voice hard with distrust.
>
> "He's just a madman who'll eloquently blabber whatever you've gone over with him. You've committed no murder, Taka."
>
> "How can you be so sure? Look at the blood all over me, Mitsu. Go see the corpse the ex-members of the football team carried to her house. . . ."
>
> "I'm sure she's dead, and with her head bashed in, sorry to say. But you didn't commit the crime intentionally. You're not capable of such an act. . . . She must have died in an accident."
>
> "Tomorrow morning when those outraged flies of the valley come to arrest me, Gii the hermit will tell them what happened. Don't fantasize, just ask him," Takashi continued to make his plea. . . .
>
> "Do you think the people of the valley who've dealt with his madness for ten-odd years will believe the madman's testimony?" As I said this, for the first time I pitied this willing murderer adamantly clinging to his immature fabrications. (220/225–26)

Mitsusaburo's refusals to accept Takashi's eyes, to let Takashi play the sacrificial lamb, and to regard Takashi as the "reincarnation" of the great-grandfather's younger brother, indirectly drive Takashi to suicide. However, the reader is not quite convinced of the older brother's terrible sense of guilt and self-incrimination vis-à-vis Takashi's suicide, which precipitates the reopening of Takashi's case and Mitsusaburo's "retrial." Apart from his cynical, distrustful, and apathetic personality, which clashed intellectually with Takashi's violent world, there seems to be no real reason for Mitsusaburo to put himself on trial except a sense of total helplessness at having failed to prevent the suicide.

The careful construction of the narrative discourse in *Manen*, which is maintained by the "debate," conceals another contest between the two brothers on a different level, however; this in the end incriminates Mitsusaburo. This contest originates in the sale of and payment for the storehouse and land which Takashi concealed from Mitsusaburo. This is a breach of trust between the two brothers. In the beginning Takashi tried to share with Mitsusaburo everything he experienced, thought about, or imagined, including what he later calls "the truth" (*hontō no koto*), i.e., his incestuous relationship with his little sister who committed suicide. However, he failed to consult with his older brother about the sale of the storehouse. Believing that he has a perfect sibling relationship, Mitsusaburo feels he is in Takashi's confidence until he accidentally learns of the sale from the assistant to the village headman:

> "Mitsusaburo, you've sold the storehouse and the land, it must have been a pretty good deal!"
> "It's not official yet. We have to think about Jin's family, and we probably won't sell the land."
> "No need to hide it from me! Must've been a damn good deal, yessir!" the assistant persisted. "Takashi and the supermarket manager have completed the registration of the sale of the land and the buildings at the office, I know most of the details, yessir!" (132/132)

This incident shows that Mitsusaburo, the titular head of the Nedokoro family, has had his role usurped and is being mocked by the village and his own brother.[5] Mitsusaburo bitterly tells us how he has been deceived:

> As I look back now, when Takashi, who had just come back from America, ambushed me as I woke up from a bad dream screaming, and said,
> —— You've got to start a new life, Mitsu. Give up everything you're doing in Tokyo, why don't you come with me to Shikoku? It's not a bad start for a new life, Mitsu! That was when the village in the valley had been restored as a reality inside me for the first time in more than ten years. And I came back to the valley to look for my own "thatched hut." However, I had been taken in by the unforeseen gloom Takashi had accumulated during his vagrancy in America like the grime on his skin. My "new life" in the valley was only meant to be a ploy for Takashi to forestall my refusal, and to sell the storehouse and the land without mishap for the sake of the something into which he was pouring his mysterious passion. The valley had never existed for me from the beginning of the journey. (133–34/134)

After this incident, we learn indirectly that Mitsusaburo secretly harbors a grudge against Takashi: he neglects to inform the reader and Takashi of one crucial piece of information which he withholds until after Takashi's death. In chapter 10, "The Riot of Imagination," the young village priest gives Mitsusaburo "the documents left by the Nedokoros for safekeeping." They are the five letters that belonged to his great-grandfather's younger brother and a pamphlet entitled "The Outcome of the Peasants' Uprising in Ōkubo Village," signed with the great-grandfather's name. The uprising recorded in the pamphlet is not the Manengannen uprising, but another one which broke out in the fourth year of Meiji (1871). Mitsusaburo tells us in detail the contents of the five letters, but not of the pamphlet. Nor does he call Takashi's attention to the documents. We know from the last chapter of the novel that he had read the entire pamphlet six chapters earlier: "I came across one peculiar account in 'The Outcome of the Ōkubo Village Peasants' Uprising' at the time when the young priest had brought the documents" (255/260). In an account written from the viewpoint of the masses, "a narrative account, rather than a historical record, of the [1871] uprising," Mitsusaburo had read the description of the leader who negotiated with the authority as the "chief representative": it talks about "a hulk of a man, we know not from where, over six feet with shaggy hair"; again, it observes, "We've already mentioned this mysterious man with shaggy hair, a real wonderous pale-faced titan, towering over six feet with a hunchback, quite misshapen, yet people were simply amazed by his eloquence as he surpassed everybody in everything." The narrator tells us that "the final account referred to him": "On the sixteenth at the entrance of the Ōkubo village as soon as he broke up the band, the firebrand of the rioters vanished into thin air" (256/262).

For the first time Mitsusaburo tells us what he had learned six chapters earlier: there were two peasants' uprisings, the Manengannen uprising and another one in 1871, both led by the same person.

> The hulk of a man with a slight stoop and his face white as a ghost was our great-grandfather's younger brother, who continued to meditate on the Manengannen uprising for ten years, confined himself in the cellar of the storehouse and suddenly reappeared on the earth. He put everything he had learned in his days of self-criticism into the second uprising. He successfully pushed it onward, making it totally different from the first uprising, which was bloody and unproductive: no one was put to death, not one single rioter or spectator dead or wounded, the second uprising

drove with effectiveness the target of attack, the Chief Councilor, to suicide. (256/263)

This astonishing finding should have been the substance of yet another round of debate between the two brothers, which would have revealed the integrity and real identity of the great-grandfather's younger brother. Why is it that Mitsusaburo did not share his discovery with Takashi? Why did he not call Takashi's attention to this crucial piece of information? Three possible reasons may be given for the narrator's "hush-up." First, he might have considered the mysterious man in the popular account unimportant. This is highly unlikely because it is Mitsusaburo's obsession, as much as Takashi's, to piece together all the information concerning the Manengannen uprising and the roles played by the great-grandfather and his younger brother. We know that Mitsusaburo used to correspond with a local historian on this issue, and in the village he continues to discuss it with the young priest of the village temple, who offers his own theory on the uprising. Secondly, there might be a narrative reason. From the narrative point of view, narrative information "has its degrees: the narrative can furnish the reader with more or fewer details. . . . The narrative can also choose to regulate the information it delivers."[6] Mitsusaburo's silence is a necessity for the narrative to complete the story it has started to tell.

Thirdly, if we look at it from Mitsusaburo's viewpoint, there exists a highly personal reason for his silence: "It is a question of fairness, tit-for-tat. Takashi has used and hurt me once for no reason; I will keep the finding a secret as long as I can." At the moment of this rather innocent decision, Mitsusaburo could not have imagined the tragic consequence. In the end he suffers from a terrible guilt, wondering why he has not discussed the "hulk of a man with shaggy hair" with Takashi. He has driven Takashi to suicide when he knew that his discovery meant everything to Takashi:

> Speechless, I shook my head, intoxicated by the revelation that continued to assert its existence. Within the central core of the revelation, the discovery that, after the Manengannen uprising, our great-grandfather's brother had not abandoned his comrades to their fate, that he had not set off through the forest for the New World, was already unshakable. Although unable to stop the beheading of his comrades, he had carried out his own punishment, confining himself to the cellar; a seemingly meaningless gesture it may have been, but he was never a turncoat. He continued to be the leader of the uprising. (251/257)

We have discussed Ōe's laminations of two historical periods, two pairs of brothers, and two quests in his narrative, wherein he presents a number of "strata" and levels for us to recognize; he also superimposes images of two different kinds of "pits" (*anaboko*), which are womb and grave at the same time.

The first "pit" appears in the beginning of the novel, which opens with Mitsusaburo descending into the "septic tank the workmen dug yesterday." Inside the pit, he is one of the living dead, abandoned by his only friend, his wife who is always drunk, and even his newborn baby who is an idiot. He reminisces about the events the novel will tell, connecting the dead friend to Takashi's enigmatic behavior and suicide: "On the autumn dawn when I crouched at the bottom of the pit with the dog on my lap, I could not comprehend *a certain thing* that continued to magnify each day in my friend's head and provoked him to commit suicide in a bizarre disguise, nor could I comprehend *a certain thing* to whose existence inside my kid brother's head my friend was at least able to come close. Death severs abruptly the vertical bond of understanding" (24/18).

Mitsusaburo spends "one hundred minutes" in the pit and, as he climbs back up the ladder, receives a sign from the dogwood tree: "Five centimeters above the ground, the backs of the dogwood leaves glowed in a radiant scarlet, terrorizing and familiar, a scorching red hue like the flames in the hell screen (which had been donated by my great-grandfather after the unfortunate incident of the Manengannen) I had seen on the Buddha's Birthday at the temple in my village in the valley. As I accepted a sign from the dogwood, its significance not yet clear, I said, Good, to myself" (27/21). This narrative beginning of *Manen* does not have an end until Mitsusaburo decodes the sign. Thirteen chapters later, at the moment of the decipherment of the mysterious code, Ōe superimposes the first pit, the septic tank, upon the second pit, the unearthed cellar which has been buried in the storehouse for one hundred years. The narrative discourse jumps in one leap from the first chapter to the last, between which the story of *Manen* narrates a series of events that have occurred over a period of twelve months. Ōe achieves a sense of this simultaneity in these two chapters by the use in both of the device of the "narrative present."

In both chapters, the first and the last, each dialogue, reproduced in flashback by the narrator, is indicated by a long dash at the beginning. These dialogues are distinguished from the "quotation-marked" dialogues narrated by Mitsusaburo. In chapter 1 we see him mourning in the pit for his dead friend who looked like a twin brother; this narrative event is repeated in the last chapter. Mitsusaburo crawls into another pit, the cellar, mourning for the death of his kid brother who took his own life: "Just as I spent time hugging my knees that autumn dawn last year in the pit for a septic tank in the backyard, I'm now sitting stockstill in a stone chamber unearthed and made a reality for earthlings by the Emperor of the supermarket and his vassals who came to conduct a preliminary survey for the dismantling of the storehouse. Across the inner room where I'm sitting is an anteroom with a privy and a well, enough for one person to live in self-confinement" (241/246). This "narrative present" produces the same cinematic effect of simultaneity demonstrated, for example, in *The Wizard of Oz*: 1) the heroine gets lost in the whirlwind of a tornado, 2) she takes a long journey to the land of Oz, 3) she wakes up from a dream and finds herself at her "home sweet home." The story of the film is the little girl's journey to Oz; while the story unfolds, the first and the third scenes remain immobile although a certain amount of time has passed between them. This passage of time is irrelevant to the story of the narrative presented in the film. Likewise, between the one-hundred-minute pit dwelling and the midnight meditation in the cellar, one year goes by. It is as if Mitsusaburo had not left the two-pits-in-one at all, the only difference being the role he plays: the receiver of the sign in the first pit, and the decoder of the sign in the second.

Central to the mysterious sign in these two narrative sequences is the color imagery of red: Mitsusaburo witnesses the red hue on five different occasions: 1) the vermilion (*shuiro*) painted on the entire head of the dead friend, 2) the burning red hue (*moeruyōna aka*) of the backs of the dogwood leaves, 3) the river of fire in the hell screen at the village temple, 4) the dead brother, Takashi, who "resembled a life-size bright red [*makka na*] plaster-of-Paris statue clad only in trousers"; 5) the blazing red sky (*moetatsu aka*) at sunrise seen from the cellar.

These clues are absolutely crucial for the understanding of the message or code. Prior to the decipherment of the sign, Mitsusaburo picks up just such a crucial clue that will aid his decoding. He visits the village temple where he reinterprets the meaning of the hell screen with the young priest:

——If your speculation is correct, this hell screen was commissioned by your great-grandfather for his own brother who was already living in the cellar, the young priest said.

> I was visited by the same profound solace as when I saw the hell screen with Takashi and my wife, this time not as a passive impression evoked by my sentiments but as a pictorial essence that existed independent of me. In the composition of the picture was an intense ''gentleness'' that had a life of its own. The commissioner of the painting had probably asked the artist to portray the very essence of ''gentleness'' in its extremity. Of course it had to depict a hell. The painting was meant for the repose of his brother's soul as he confronted, while still alive, his own solitary inferno in self-confinement. The river of fire had to be as red as the backs of dogwood leaves in autumn flooded with the morning sunlight, and the undulations of the waves of fire had to be drawn in lines soft and gentle as the folds of a woman's flowing kimono. The very ''gentleness'' of the river of fire had to be there. . . . (258/264–65)

At the moment of the denouement, the narrator and the reader are able to move from one stratum of red imagery to another as we pass from one level of the story to the next. As if in a series of transparencies placed together, we are given a total picture of the mysterious sign:

> The forest that filled in most of the space left by the tearing down of the wall lay pitch-black, shrouded in layers of mist, only the dim grape halo reflected the twilight sky, and just above the right-hand corner the fiery red sky was visible. When I greeted that particular morning, lurking in the pit in the backyard, and saw the same burning red hue on the backs of the dogwood leaves, the image of the hell screen in the hollow [the village] was recreated in my mind; I felt as though I had received a sign. Now I can easily interpret the sign whose significance was yet unclear at that time. The ''gentleness'' of this red in the hell screen is a balm to help them forget the terrifying threats of those tormented ones who face their own hell head-on and overcome it, this hue itself is for the consolation of those who try quietly to live through a semidark, unstable, obscure reality. (263–64/271)

What is in the end transmitted to the reader is this: the process of decipherment requires two people, Takashi and Mitsusaburo. Takashi continually fails in action, but what he says, i.e., what he wanted to believe about the great-grandfather's younger brother, turns out to be true. Mitsusaburo fails in what he says, but not in what he does. His one-hundred-minute pit dwelling proves to be the symbolic reenactment of the great-grandfather's younger brother's self-confinement in the cellar. Takashi points to the truth; Mitsusaburo by his symbolic act reveals its content.

Manen, the tale of "one hundred years," therefore, simultaneously explores two quests, one individual, the other collective: quests for the meaning both of an individual death and of its relationship to history as a series of cumulative violent transgressions. Haunted by his friend's death, Mitsusaburo takes up the position of an antiheroic bystander, a survivor, who pursues his private intellectual quest in isolation. Takashi, a heroic activist, tries passionately and violently to become a part of human reality, a "clamp" that holds two different historical periods together in simultaneity. In the end, however, the two quests merge into one in the suicide of Takashi, which reveals to Mitsusaburo the answer he has been seeking: "The light of our great-grandfather's brother's identity illuminates a new picture: that the suicide of Takashi, who had lived only to copy the life of his great-grandfather's brother, was the sublime ultimate adventure by which Takashi flaunted before me, the survivor, the entirety of his 'truth' " (261/268). Mitsusaburo, the model reader of *Manen*, and Ōe in the end share the same worldview. Ōe once said in reference to the composition of *Manen*: "Only by thinking that my own flesh that will be dead someday will live on, intimately bound up with history and today's reality, am I released from the fear of death."[7]

*   *   *

Manen also belongs to a series of works in which Ōe focuses on the kind of relationships experienced by the two brothers, whose native village is in a valley on Shikoku: the growing-up of the pair in perfect harmony in "Prize Stock," and the disintegration of the bond between the two in *Nip the Buds, Gun the Kids*.[8] In *The Youth Who Came in Late* each brother goes his own way, with the older brother left to face the world alone. In light of this theme of the adventures of the two brothers, we can see *Manen* as a "requiem" composed by the older brother for his younger brother who had experienced the "sublime ultimate adventure" on behalf of Mitsusaburo. With *Manen* Ōe temporarily concludes his tale of the two brothers.[9]

While Ōe explores the world of the two brothers who are an entirely new pair in each story, he sets them against major historical periods and events: winter 1944 (during the war), summer 1945 (the end of the war), the 1950s (American Occupation), the 1960s (Ampo demonstrations). What is the significance of these works upon which Ōe bases the paradigm of the older brother vs. the younger brother? He had the choice of writing a saga of the brothers and tracing the chronological development of their involvement with and reactions to sociopolitical changes that swept Japan between 1944 and 1967. However, the adherence to the same pair of brothers would have restricted Ōe in experimenting with multifaceted and multilayered texts, because all of the biographical data concerning the pair would have to be coordinated as Ōe continued to write about them. He frees himself from the limitations of the techniques of biography or a historical novel, which would not allow him to experiment with "continuity in discontinuity." *Manen*, a narrative of simultaneity, an attempt to look simultaneously at the linear movement of historical events, foreshadows Ōe's ambitious undertaking to combine the functions of simultaneity and contemporaneity in the novel he wrote thirteen years later.

6

The Device of Repetition: In Quest of Dialogic Narrative

"Father, Where Are You Going?" (Chichi yo, anata wa doko e ikuno ka?, 1968, hereafter "Father"), "Teach Us To Outgrow Our Madness" (Warera no kyōki o ikinobiru michi o oshieyo, 1969, hereafter "Teach Us"), and *The Day He Himself Shall Wipe My Tears Away* (Mizu kara waga namida o nuguitamō hi, 1971, hereafter *My Tears*) show an obsessive repetition of characters, events, images, and dialogues, sometimes repeated word for word, paragraph for paragraph. It is as though Ōe had rewritten the same draft again and again, and had found in all the versions independently satisfying stories.[1] Repetition becomes the fabric of the stories, shapes their structure, and provides an impetus to their narrative movement.

"Father, Where Are You Going?" a line taken from Blake's poem "The Little Boy Lost,"[2] opens with the confession of the narrator (whose name we are not told): "I write, [[. . . while my father spent his days in self-confinement,]] and have again realized that I have to abort the manuscript" (7).[3] This short story is a narrative of reminiscences: vague memories of the narrator's father who died suddenly in self-confinement perpetuate the narrator's desire to "recreate a whole image of his father." The narrator was stimulated to undertake the "reproduction project" because, on the one hand, he was too young to remember the details of his father's self-confinement and death and, on the other, his mother, the only capable informant, has adamantly refused to tell her son anything. She maintains total silence. This pattern becomes "the figure in the carpet" for Ōe, the overall plan that also governs the two subsequent stories, "Teach Us" and *My Tears*. As the Jamesian narrative based on the "quest for an absolute and absent cause"[4] is set in motion by the absence of knowledge, Ōe's tales are also provoked by something that is not present. The narrator/biographer talks to 1) his father, who does not see/hear/speak (=self-confinement); 2) his mother, who does not recognize her own son (=feigning); 3) his wife, who does not believe her husband (=distrust); 4) his son, who does not know language (=idiocy). "Father" tells of the father who wants to have "dialogic" contact with his own father, who ignored him in the dark storehouse, and with his own son, who is retarded, has rickets, and has never uttered a word nor run nor jumped. No dialogue is open to the narrator/biographer, who plays a double role. He [X] is at the same time a son and a father caught in between: the father of X : X : the retarded son of X. In short, "Father" is a tale of the quest for dialogic narrative, and this quest continues in "Teach Us" and *My Tears*.

Without accurate, concrete data about his father, the biography is doomed to fail. It will never be completed. Paradoxically, this limitation also makes it possible for the biographer to start the project over and over again. There is no beginning or ending, the task generates a perpetual repetition. The biographer likens himself to an archaeologist trying to recreate the entire bone structure of a dinosaur based on a fossil of a lower jaw bone. As the narration struggles to reproduce an image of the dead father, the reader must organize in his mind the sequence of incidents surrounding the self-confinement of the father, because the narrator does not give these incidents in sequential order: something triggers the mind of the biographer, who jots down whatever he feels is relevant to the project. His fragmentary notes constitute the narrative. "Sometimes when I got stuck with my project daydreaming about my father, I either wrote notes or made tape recordings, in various styles, about my reproduction plan" (8).

The repeated act of writing the biography creates the very structure of narrative discourse in "Father": "I hope my reader can bear with me; the only thing I can do is to explain step by step the entire process of this undertaking" (10). The act of repetition, however, does not end with the task of the biographer, but extends to several other elements within the story. First there is a humorous episode of recording and replaying in the dead of night a tape of an imaginary dialogue between the biographer and his wife, who is already deeply asleep in the adjoining bedroom. The biographer's recorded voice narrates one of Blake's poems, "The Little Boy Lost," which he calls paragraph "A":

A Father, father! Where Are You Going?
O do not walk so fast.
Speak, father, speak to your little boy,
Or else I shall be lost.[5] (12)

Through the stimulus of this poem, the biographer attempts to reproduce his childhood in search of a dialogue with his own father, who constantly ignored the presence of the little boy.

In the next paragraph, A', the biographer comes back to the present and plays the role of a husband in search of a dialogue with his own wife. He is suspicious that she might be a voyeur and pretends she is hiding. The resulting imaginary dialogue is recorded on the tape:

A'
Why are you peeping at your husband through the keyhole. . . . I'm simply trying to understand my father who died twenty-five years ago. You say I'm mad? It's the other way around. I'm trying not to repeat the life of a man who'd gone mad, covered his eyes and ears in self-confinement, moved his mouth only to eat and accumulated enough fat to collapse his heart. I'm investigating how he was cornered into a *cul-de-sac*. (12)

The husband then changes tactics:

A''
Hey, you should be ashamed of peeping at your husband through the keyhole. You distrust me, don't you, you think that I might be masturbating? I don't make love to you because of the hormone imbalance brought on by obesity. . . . (12–13)

Now the reader learns that the biographer is fat like his father and wants to approach his image by imitating his mad behavior. The third variation of the imaginary dialogue reveals the repetitive nature of the biographer's life: he does things by rote.

A'''
——Ha, ha, ha, ha, I knew for a long time that you've been peeping at me through the keyhole. Every year around this time, I drink whisky all night, play the tape recorder, sleep during the day, and shut myself up for a week without seeing my wife or my son, an annual event that began five years ago. . . . (13)

As the biographer repeats the task of recreating a whole image of his father, the repetition of recording and replaying his voice on a tape recorder is superimposed on the biographer's remembrance of the act of his father recording, replaying, and erasing his own voice twenty-five years ago. The distinction between the present and the past blurs, and the coexistence of THEN and NOW emerges.

The effect of these futile repetitions, as the reader can see, is comic. Another comical use of repetition with a touch of absurdity in "Father" occurs in an episode that I call "an assassin mounting several unsuccessful attacks on the father-in-self-confinement." As often happens in the story, this episode is sparked by the memory of the father's wax-cylinder recording machine, which he originally purchased in order to learn Chinese so that he could publish translations of Chinese poetry. Ōe later "recycles" this recording machine in *My Tears*, where the machine is used by the biographer's mother to describe the "worth" of the mad husband: "Taking radios and phonographs apart and putting them back together was about the one thing *a certain party* [his father] could do a pretty decent job on—he was at least average when it came to working with his hands—and he had a radio and a phonograph in the storehouse" (151/89).[6]

In "Father," at the outbreak of the war, the recording machine was confiscated by the secret police, who, in league with the villagers, spread a rumor that the narrator's father was either a lunatic or a spy who sent secret codes to the other side of the Pacific. According to the narrator's grandmother, "he was neither a spy nor a lunatic. He got involved in an incident (which happened either in China or in a big city in Japan)" (16). The assassin who assaulted the father in the dark storehouse possibly had something to do with the incident. The narrator/biographer tells us that he will select the accounts of what his grandmother told him from the manuscript he could not finish:

> Finally the assassin, consumed with fury, stood in front of the storehouse holding a drawn sword. . . . He brandished his sword, shouted at the top of his voice, yahhh, yahhh, yahhh, dashed into the storehouse, barely missing the pitiful man in meditation in the barber chair, banged himself against the clay wall, bounced around and out to where he started. As he renewed his spirits, with the drawn sword held high in the sky, he jumped right back into the storehouse yelling, yahhh, yahhh, yahhh, ran past the man in meditation who waited perfectly still for the moment of assassination, banged himself against the wall, and came out again. Some firemen and veterans caught up with the assassin in the courtyard, who had by then expended all his reserves of energy. (17)

The slapstick farce of the assassin's fruitless repetition is a self-parody of the reiteration that provokes the narrative discourse of "Father." In "Teach Us" Ōe repeats the same episode in summary as something the biographer (called the fat man) heard from his grandmother:

> His grandmother had said more than once that his father had been attacked by an assassin with a Japanese sword, and that he managed to escape harm by sitting perfectly still in the dark storehouse without offering any resistance. The assassin was probably one of the band which had been associated with his father through the junior officers in the revolt. . . . He [the assassin] tracked down a craven like himself to the place where he [the fat man's father] was living in self-confinement, and brandished his Japanese sword and threatened emptily, but that was all he had ever intended to do. (85/217)[7]

The end of "Father" suggests that the narrator's repetition might not be futile, when the receptive act is contrasted with the sequence in which the retarded son runs for the first time. The son of a fat madman who covered his eyes and ears and sat stock-still in a barber chair, the biographer is also the father of a physically handicapped son who has not yet uttered a single word. The father leaves the son on top of a slope and runs down the hill, repeatedly calling the boy's name. He runs back and forth over and over again. The son stands perfectly still. The father repeats the act. "What if I have a heart attack on the spot? How will my son react? In that brain shrouded in the mist of dullness, what sort of reaction will emerge, take shape, and explode? Father, father! Where are you going?/O do not walk so fast/Speak, father speak to me,/or else I shall be lost" (46).

After countless attempts, the father witnesses the successful result: for the first time the boy runs down the hill like "a normal human being" toward his panting father, who is writhing on his back in the grass. The narrative discourse in the story comes to a halt when the repetition produces a desirable effect. In a roundabout manner, then, the father and the son discover how to communicate with each other and make dialogic contact without the means of verbal communication. The self-parody of repetition suddenly takes on a serious tone at the end of the story. Because the son/father sees some kind of significance in his repeated act, he decides not to abandon the "reproduction project" for the moment:

My father . . .]] I began to write all over again. When I recognize clearly what the purpose is for writing it, the biography of my father will be either completed or abandoned totally. [[My father began his retreat from the world because. . . . (47)

The oxtail stew episode also suggests that repetition can produce successful dialogue. Like the episode in which "an assassin attacks the father-in-self-confinement," Ōe recycles the "oxtail stew" episode only twice. That is to say, the former episode is repeated in "Father" and "Teach Us" but not in *My Tears*; the latter episode in "Father" and *My Tears* but not in "Teach Us." In "Father" the verbal assault the narrator's mother directs against his father's uncontrollable appetite again triggers a memory: "Appetite was my father's weakest point. . ." (40). The oxtail stew anecdote is already twice removed from the actual incident because the narrator gives an account of what his older brothers have told him. It goes like this: one day there was an illegal killing of an ox in the village. One of the narrator's brothers represented the family and went out to get a share of the kill. The villagers discriminated against the little boy, giving him only half a thigh and a tail. All night he was lost and by the time he returned home, there was only a tail in the sack. "My father made one of his rare appearances outside the storehouse to do the cooking of oxtail stew, which he had learned during his stay in China, and stood in the kitchen in the main house to confront a piece of oxtail with black hide, hair and all" (41).

When the narrator himself cooks an oxtail stew his act is a means by which he captures the lost time and becomes one with his dead father. Total identification and assimilation takes place: "diachronic" time is obliterated. In the guise of a gourmet cook, "I wear sunglasses," just as his father did, "with a pretext that they are useful as protection against the spattering from the joints of oxtail heated in lard" (41). The cooking session turns into a ritual for the biographer to reproduce the image of his father. In *My Tears*, in the process of recycling the material, Ōe gives an expanded, more detailed version of how the son/narrator helps his fat father cook the stew—the first occasion his father ever addresses the little boy.

But "Father" contains another story which, in the context of the other narratives, contradicts this hopeful message. Structurally, in addition to the two tales, the one dealing with the biographer's father-in-self-confinement and the other with the little boy's success in running, the third tale that dovetails with "Teach Us" concerns the biographer/

narrator's "date" with a transvestite. This humorous story within a story plays upon the two-in-one role of the son/father narrator. A French transvestite had taken a fancy to the narrator at a conference held in New York City some years before. During a subsequent visit a few years later, the narrator runs into the transvestite. He insists on referring to the transvestite, whose appearance and behavior exhibit femininity *in toto*, as "she (he)." But in actuality "she" is a "he": the presence of a female, yet the substance of a male. The identity as a male is exposed accidentally when the narrator grabs her (his) erect penis which he mistakes for the car's emergency brake! They wander into the Museum of Modern Art where she (he) points out the striking resemblance the narrator bears to a sculpture of a plaster-of-Paris man seated on a bus driver's seat turned away from the viewer. The biographer/narrator is immediately infatuated with the piece and buys a postcard of a plaster-of-Paris man about to straddle a bicycle, by the same sculptor. The side-long view of the man reminds him of his own father, who sat on a barber chair in the dark; even in the photograph his face is forever turned away from the viewer.

The picture card becomes part and parcel of the biographer's life, one more clue that might solve the mystery of his father's self-confinement and death. At the end of "Teach Us," however, the fat man, defeated by his mother who blocks his "reconstruction project," burns a sheaf of pages "which contained every word he had written down about his father" (85–86/218) and the "picture card which had been thumbed-tacked above his desk since he had brought it back from New York, of a sculpture, a plaster-of-Paris man who resembled his father as he fancied him, about to straddle a plaster-of-Paris bicycle" (86/218).

My Tears is the most complicated text in its repetitions. It takes up a subject introduced by an earlier series of repetitions. Among the incidents that appear in all the works under discussion, "his mother's accusatory silence and the ensuing verbal assault" gives an excellent example of the circularity of Ōe's narrative. We learn in "Father" that the biographer is not on speaking terms with his mother, who lives in the deep forest lands of Shikoku Island. "My mother, who had never criticized or reminisced about my father since his death (that was why I came up with the idea to recreate his image based on the fossils of memory, or a desire to write his biography which I have continued until now), suddenly broke her silence and began to criticize me and my father" (25).

However, she does not reproach her son directly, but only indirectly, through his wife, who becomes the intermediary in the war of nerves between the mother and the son. In a telephone conversation with the wife, the mother remarks on her son's suicide attempt the previous morning:

> ——That child knows he's not doing anything in earnest, it's a waste of time to worry about him. His father was just like that.
> ——I'm sure he's not in earnest; he's eating oatmeal with a big grin on his face.
> . . .
> ——The child's father repeated what he knew was fake. Since he wasn't in earnest, he couldn't experience anything real, or find out what kind of effect it had on him . . . when he realized what he was doing, it was too late. What stupidity! (25)

The narrator's wife relays to him his mother's version of what caused his father to withdraw, which the narrator then "reproduces" for the reader. In other words, I (the narrator) am telling you (the reader) that my wife said that my mother said to tell me:

> ——Your mother asked me never to take you seriously, my wife said, if you started glorifying your father's behavior during his last years. If you try to justify his behavior by arguing that he sat perfectly still in the storehouse wearing pitch-black sunglasses and ear plugs because he wanted to deny the reality of a world in which Japan was making war on China, she said, it is true that he spent his last years sitting in a storehouse without moving, with his eyes and ears covered, but it was simply madness that made him do what he did, not a protest against the times. He had been as fat as a pig when he died because he had been stuffing himself with everything he could lay hands on without moving anything but his mouth, and your mother asked me to tell you, he had probably hidden himself in that storehouse because he was ashamed of being the only fat man around at a time when food was scarce. (40)

This battle between the mother and the son is carried on in "Teach Us." The son's defense against his mother's accusations, however, deteriorates quickly because she has stolen his manuscript and notes in which he has invested so much time and effort. "This produced a new repetition of collisions with his mother, who had never spoken about his father's self-confinement and death and had combatted him for years for pretending to go mad whenever he questioned her. Not only did she refuse to cooperate; during a stay at his home while he was traveling abroad she had stolen his notes and incomplete manuscript for a biography of his father and retained them to this day" (55/177–78). On the telephone the fat man/biographer confronts his mother and repeats her accusations against him by *retelling* what she has told his wife (which we know from "Father") word for word:

> . . . Didn't you ask my wife not to take "sonny boy" seriously if he started glorifying his father's behavior during his last years? . . . didn't you tell my wife not to believe for a minute that he's done that as a protest against the times, because he wanted to deny the reality of a world in which Japan was making war on the China he revered? Didn't you tell her it was simply madness that made him do what he did? Didn't you even say that Father had been as fat as a pig when he died because he'd been stuffing himself with everything he could lay hands on without moving anything but his mouth, and then insinuate that he had hidden himself in that storehouse because he was ashamed of being the only fat man around at a time when food was so scarce? . . . That morning my wife had the illusion I was about to hang myself, you told her my father was never in earnest; that he knew everything he did was fake, because he told himself he was not in earnest whenever he began something, but he didn't notice the effect it was actually having on him however little at a time, wasn't conscious of it, and that it was too late when he did notice. . . . (80–81/211–12)

Now the vituperation has been presented in a full circle with the flow of "communication" fixed rigidly in one direction:

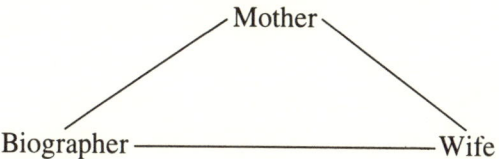

As a result of this renewed battle, the mother discloses another explanation, probably an authentic one, of the cause of his father's self-confinement. She sends a printed notice to his wife: "I am reminded that my late husband, having had an acquaintance with the officers involved in a certain coup d'état, was led upon failure to the dreadful conclusion that no course of action remained but the assassination of his Imperial Majesty. It was the horror of this which moved him to confine himself in a storehouse, where he remained until his death" (84/215).

This "certain coup d'état" is recycled in all three of the stories. It first appears in "Father" in a dream the biographer often has. The dream takes the form of a play which he either watched as a boy or heard from his older brothers, or possibly from his grandmother. In the dream, the nameless drama, in commemoration of the thirty-five-year anniversary of a coup d'état, is played by the aged widows of junior officers of the Imperial Army who were executed for their part in the revolt. There is a "man seated in a huge chair with his back to the widows, now thirty-five years younger, who stalk behind him with drawn daggers" (20). The chair looks like "the barber chair my father sat in during his last years" or "a throne of a king." Is the man "the highest Authority to have abandoned the young junior officers, or a private citizen who sympathized politically, provided funds, and was generally in league with the junior officers until the day of the revolt, finally betrayed them, dropped out of the uprising, and spent what remained of his life hiding in a storehouse in his country village?" (20). In "Teach Us" the drama, the fat man's fondest dream since his youth, mystifies the true identity of his father, who might have been, in the fat man's reveries, "the highest Authority" or "a private citizen" conspiring to assassinate the Imperial Majesty. The dream-turned-into reality is what constitutes the theme of *My Tears*. To ascertain the role his father played in the coup d'état, the validity of the coup, and the role of the divine Emperor, the little boy continues "his appeal for opening a dialogue" with his mother.

A personal quest for a dialogue, which starts in "Father" and continues in "Teach Us," expands into something more public in *My Tears*, shifting from the individual issue (of a private citizen) to that of the collective (the highest Authority, i.e., the Emperor). The fat man/biographer in "Teach Us" learns through the intermediary that his mother scornfully refers to his father only as "the man" (*ano hito*), whereas the narrator of *My Tears* prefers the designation (it is still *ano hito* in the original, though "*a certain party*" is John Nathan's translation), since it is "a way of exalting him into a kind of idol" (123/50). The deliberate ambivalence Ōe imparts to the term *ano hito* is significant because "the man," although it originally referred to his father, also means "the Man," the divine Emperor, who was never on public view and was never referred to by name.

My Tears repeats events, as the earlier narratives do. The entire text consists of a "repeating narrative,"[8] narrating *n* times what happened once. The same event is told several times, not only with stylistic variations but also with additional information that can be brought together and in the end interpreted by the reader. The same principal of narrative frequency operates in the production of "Father" and "Teach Us," that is, Ōe repeats the same event—which happened once— intertextually as well as internally.

The story (the "what" of narrative) in *My Tears* is of a thirty-five-year-old man, dying of liver cancer, who tells what he thinks happened to his father-in-self-confinement on August 15, 1945. The narrative or discourse (the "way" of narrative) takes, depending on the viewpoint of the reader and the narrator, one or all of the forms of confession, testimony, chronicle (a "history of the age"), allegory, and memoir. Narration is produced by the "dying" man who narrates an event of twenty-five years ago, which is recorded by the scribe, his wife (also treated as the nurse), and contradicted and discredited by his mother.

Ōe also employs the literary technique of "laying bare," which has been analyzed by Russian formalists: "a perceptible device is permissible only when it is made creatively outstanding. When a device is noticed despite the author's attempt to conceal it, it produces a detrimentally comic effect. To prevent this, the author deliberately lays bare the device."[9] Ōe lays bare the techniques of narration and composition. We are constantly reminded of the presence of the scribe, who objects to the narrator's choice of words, gives uninvited suggestions, asks questions, and in the end is relieved of her position as the "acting executor of the will." We are not supposed to know that a work of verbal art is actually being recorded by someone; we are expected to believe the story to be "completed," not a draft being produced right in front of us. The complexity and the strangeness of the text are further compounded by 1) infidelities to the chronological order of events; 2) repetition, or narrative frequency;[10] 3) a fluidity in the use of personal pronouns; 4) the elimination of direct quotation marks.

As is the case with "Father" and "Teach Us," the opening passage of *My Tears* has no bearing at all on the chronological order of narrated events of the following pages. What the narrator believes happened, what he imagined happened, what he wants to remember, are given in a piecemeal fashion. The first five paragraphs give us extremely limited information: he (we do not know who) is someone with liver cancer in a hospital bed, wears tinted underwater goggles, and encounters at midnight a Dharma-like creature, who resembles *a certain party*. Not only do we not know who this *he* is, but we are not sure that the what of the narrative (the story) has any beginning at all, apart from the fact *he* apparently has something to do with *a certain party*. (Even halfway through the text we cannot improve on this observation.) The sixth paragraph abruptly solves the mystery of *who* he is: "[[Must I put down even that kind of silliness? asks the 'acting executor of the will,' who is taking down his verbal account" (89/4). At this moment we know bare facts: that *he* is the narrator, and that someone else is recording his words, which are the sum total of the what of the narrative, *My Tears*.

The incidents surrounding *a certain party* illustrate the temporal distortions that violate the chronological order of events. Although *he* knows *a certain party*, we do not know the relationship between the two, nor the identity of *a certain party* until we are sixty pages into the text. Scattered throughout the narrative is the following information (the number before each sentence indicates the sequential order of what we are accustomed to in a realistic presentation of a story like the one told by Marlow in *Heart of Darkness*):

1. His mother also knows *a certain party* (92/8).

8. *A certain party's* underwater goggles have been given to *him* (92/8).

7. *A certain party* had been killed in a street battle (92/8).

6. Ten soldiers came and asked *a certain party* to join them (103/22).

5. *He* used to sleep with *a certain party* in the storehouse (121/47).

4. *A certain party* had shut himself up in the storehouse (121/47).

2. The scribe suggests calling *a certain party* "father" (123/49).

3. *He* is the real son of *a certain party* (131/61).

Five pages before the end of the story, we think *he* knows that the Dharma-like creature *he* encountered in the beginning of the story is his mother. However, again we are not sure when exactly she comes into the room and sits at the foot of his bed. Instead of unentangling all the Gordian knots, Ōe either tightens them or creates additional "snares."[11] To use Ōe's metaphor, the way (discourse) of the narrative continues, like cancer, with cell-by-cell proliferation, or, like the overcooked oxtail stew, all the secret ingredients are meshed together and it is the reader's task to burrow his way gingerly through them. While the narrative discourse proliferates, bifurcates at each juncture, layers one incident on top of another, or dovetails one with another, it continuously repeats an event that happened only once.

The tortuosity of Ōe's narrative also originates in the carefree use of personal pronouns. Characters are not designated by one particular personal pronoun. The narrator refers to himself sometimes in the first person, sometimes in the third person. His story is challenged by *she*, the scribe, and by the ultimate executor, *she*, his mother. The narrative is a mixture of "reported" and "immediate" speech alternating with "narratized" discourse. In "reported" speech the narrator "pretends literally to give the floor to his character."[12] "——A wagon! You call that ridiculous box on top of the two sawed-off logs a wagon, his mother said unsparingly" (120/46). In "immediate" speech the narrator is "obliterated and the character *substitutes* for him."[13] In "narratized" discourse, which distinguishes nothing external "between what was word in the original and what was gesture, posture, state of mind,"[14] the narrator tells his own story in the third person.

For "immediate" speech, Ōe eliminates quotation marks to enhance fluidity in the use of personal pronouns and to "activate" the function of *parole* (speech act) in the narrative. The following example, a conversation between the narrator and the scribe, his wife (called the nurse), illustrates the fluidity Ōe can achieve in Japanese:[15]

> [[Once August begins, "he" is in a state of constant agitation . . . "he" repeatedly cries out as though in great danger. However, "he" insists to a dubious "acting executor of the will" that "he" continues to have no memory whatsoever of his dreams. These past few days you've frequently expressed concern over whether your mother will be able to survive the heat of this summer, I wonder if your dreams might have something to do with that? the "acting executor of the will" says. It could be, now when I'm finally in a position to really let my mother have it for the first time in my life . . . "he" replies with objective calm. . . . You and your mother promised one another you wouldn't commit suicide? When I was in high school my mother made certain I would never be able to try suicide by hurting and humiliating me so deeply my basic attitudes toward society around me were bent all out of shape. . . . (143–44/78–79)

The narrative flows, giving the reader a sensation of moving through it backward, forward, and sideways. It has the effect of "a text which takes several levels of its own 'textuality' and presents them all simultaneously."[16] By employing "repeating narrative," Ōe lets one text speak to the other, the preceding one to the following one, and vice versa. On the level of the story (the what), the narratives show the father/son in desperate struggle to open a dialogue with his parents, wife, and son. On the level of the discourse, one narrative (or one text) attests to "an absorption of and a reply to another text,"[17] one in a constant dialogue with another.

Another kind of repetition in this narrative is the allusion to mythic figures, which functions paradoxically. As Ōe "rewrites" "Father" and "Teach Us," the emphasis shifts from the son (the biographer) trying to relate to his father to the father (the biographer) trying to relate to his idiot son. In *My Tears* Ōe goes one step further and layers three polysemic relationships of father/son or master/subject one on top of the other: 1) Don Quixote/Sancho Panza; 2) the Divine Emperor/His children; 3) God/Christ.

My Tears, sharing the upside-down world of *Don Quixote*, is a masterpiece of parody, a long-neglected genre in Japan. Inoue Hisashi, one of the few satirists in Japan, draws upon oxymoron to define parody as "an accurately distorted mirror." It debases the value of an object by accurately imitating it but at the same time distorting it. Its main task is to search for a similarity, however weak, between the great and the insignificant and to identify the two.[18] Another definition of parody calls into play the archaic religious conception of "the second aspect" or the "double." For example, servants and jesters imitate and caricature the protagonist in a story and become doubles of the hero himself. "This idea of doubling . . . constitutes the nature of all parody. We encounter it, without exception, 'paired': without chiaroscuro, without something to be contrasted to something else, it does not exist."[19]

My Tears is filled with images and situations "paired" and "contrasted": the obese "infant" father is nursed by his skinny "maternal" son; the mother loves her stepson and rejects her real son; while the father has his real son shot, the stepmother wants the deserter stepson to escape; the son dreads his mother's hateful sideways glances while he is ready to settle for even one cursory glance which his father never gives; the ten-year-old boy wears adult clothes and rides on an adult bicycle. The only way the little boy can ride this bicycle is by "side-pedaling," and Ōe stresses the fact that the size of the vehicle is a "number 8." This number, a visual manifestation of two circles "paired," represents the two wheels of the bicycle, the two round black lenses of the underwater goggles that cover the eyes of *a certain party* and the narrator, and the two dreadful eyes of the narrator's mother.

The ten-year-old son, paired with his fat father dying of bladder cancer, is a watchman, nursemaid, waiter, henchman, soldier—in short, a little factotum. The master/father, embodying everything from quixotic madness to gargantuan excess, has one mission to carry out: "... We're going to steal ten fighter planes from the army field and disguise them to look like American planes and bomb the Imperial palace. There's no other way left to make the Japanese people rise up and protect the true essence of our nation!" (156/96). Deprived of a white horse to mount, the only transportation available to him and his little soldier and drunken subjects is a cart, "a ridiculous wooden fertilizer box with sawed-off legs for wheels," lined with pillows and old diapers.

Ōe's Sancho Panza, born too late to join the Imperial Army and fight for the divine Emperor, finds in the "tub of lard" a substitute for the human Emperor. This substitute addresses the little boy, asking him to support his enormous weight back to the storehouse after the ritual of the oxtail stew cooking session is over. Ōe cheerfully appropriates a Rabelaisian gaiety and farce in a phallic and urinary rhapsody: "Slowly they advanced toward the entrance to the storehouse, but *a certain party's* feet, ponderously lifting and lowering like the leg of a circus elephant stepping up onto a barrel, simply could not step across the broad, high threshold of the many-layered fire door. And when the boy dropped to his knees on the ground that retained the midday warmth and threw his arms around the calf of the thick pole of a leg *a certain party* was still laboring patiently to lift and tried to lend him strength, *a certain party* fell over on his back as unceremoniously as an infant but with a thud that shook the ground. Then his large, pitch-black penis sprang from the long-since buttonless fly of his 'people's' overalls, and he energetically urinated" (140/74).

The image of the human Emperor, the fat father, becomes increasingly imbued with the authority of God addressing his only son, Christ: "... *a certain party* faced his chosen son and spoke as follows, heedless of the enemy firing into him, Have you seen what must be seen? For the next quarter-century that you will live remember always what you have seen. All has been accomplished, you have seen what must be seen, Survive and remember, that is your role, Do nothing else!" (159/101). This is his Lord for whom the little boy secretly sheds blood: "Please drink the blood; it is for you!" (109/27).

The narrative also includes parodies of other literary texts—including Ōe's own. Unable to restrain himself from parodying his own earlier works and one of the holiest haiku by Bashō about a frog and an ancient pond, Ōe lays bare the literary device of a so-called 5-7-5 form and purposely blocks our *automatic* response to and perception of the traditional form. The narrator's father, as a representative of the "Manchurian Committee to Revere Bashō the Master," composes a doggerel about a frog (*kawazu* in classical Japanese and *kaeru* in modern Japanese, which also means "to change," "to return," and is often used with other verbs to form compounds). Ōe puns on *kaeru*:

> What is a frog?
> It is hatching eggs
> It is exchanging for money
> It is a pompous ass sitting back
> It is being knocked down flat on its back
> It is returning to an old garden
> It is returning to mud
> It is everything quieting down
> Many of these belong to human reality.
> The old pond—/A frog leaps in,/And a splash.[20] (125/53)

At another time, the narrator parodies Ōe's own work, alluding to the two hundred dogs that appear in "A Strange Job," *The Youth Who Came in Late*, etc.:

> Once he was awake he could hear that not only the patient next door but the two hundred dogs kept in the hospital courtyard for use in the laboratory had also been threatened by his sobbing and clearly were howling still; nonetheless, he thought to himself, I am only dreaming; besides, I'm fully conscious of the significance of those howling dogs because I've written about them, this is no time for howling dogs." (99–100/18)

On another occasion, a famous classical work is the object of parody. According to the narrator's mother, *a certain party's* last words, "All has been accomplished, you have seen what must be seen," that echo the Biblical prophecy, are the quotation her real father found in the *Tale of the Heike* "when he read it in prison and sent it to relatives that were about to be bereaved, yessir! Can you imagine *a certain party* turning to a pitiful little child and speaking to him in classical Japanese?" (160/102).

The effect of these parodic repetitions is what Russian formalists called "defamiliarization" of literary techniques. Victor Shklovsky defines "defamiliarization" as the de-automatization of perception and the habitual way of thinking: "And so it is in order to restore the feeling of life, to be aware of things, in order to make the stone stony, that there exists what is called art. The aim of art is to give the feeling of a thing as something seen, and not as something recognized. The device of art is the device of making things strange, and the device of impeded form, which increases the difficulty and duration of perception since the process of perception in art is an end in itself and must be prolonged.''[21] Ōe "defamiliarizes" a familiar historical subject, Japan's surrender and the prewar relationship between Japanese and the divine Emperor, by presenting it through the eyes of a ten-year-old boy superimposed on the eyes of the grown-up man, who still believes in the myth of the Emperor System, his "Happy Days."

Finally, the "one event" narrated *n* times in *My Tears* and its grave significance are laid bare: "August fifteenth, 1945, the Emperor swiftly descended to earth to announce the surrender in the voice of a mortal man. August sixteenth, his Majesty circling upward in a swift ascent again . . . would revive as the national essence itself, and more certainly than before, more divinely, as a ubiquitous chrysanthemum, would cover Japan and all her people. As a golden chrysanthemum illuminated from behind by a vast purple light and glittering like an aurora, his Majesty would manifest himself" (157/98–99). The hallucinatory ecstasy that overwhelms the thirty-five-year-old son is "contrasted" with the "chill objectivity" and "negative evidence" presented by his mother, who discredits her son's memories, those memories he wants to remember. This contrast reminds us that the narrated event may not have happened the way the narrator tells us: ". . . there's no telling whether I've actually experienced what I say, correspondence with reality in itself has never meant anything anyway, 'he' says" (97/14). The reader has already suspected that this narrative by a man possibly mad, possibly dying of liver cancer, may be unreliable; this passage suggests that the narrator suspects his own reliability. Imagining is a "supreme game" he enjoys; he is often unable to deny his mother's account, which has "a reasonably combative correctness." He sometimes doubts "if I hadn't created *a certain party* entirely in my imagination" (123/50). In passages like this, the narrator suggests that to argue what may or may not be true, what may or may not be realistic *(nichijōteki)*, is outside the realm of fiction or a work of verbal art. This is the point Ōe is trying to make in *My Tears*: this is his own *raison d'être* as a writer.[22]

If the narrator succumbed to his mother's imputation that he is escaping by the repeated act of remembering only what he wants to remember, to the doctor's words that he is not dying of liver cancer, or to his own misgivings that *a certain party* might be a phantom, *My Tears* would no longer be a parody. For this reason, the narrator, pitied by his mother, the contender, must continue the quixotic journey to meet "the colossal chrysanthemum topped with a purple aurora," the symbol of the Emperor, at the top of the stone steps.

*   *   *

The primary circumstance to which Ōe's parodic method responds is what he calls "the intrinsic singularity of the Japanese intellectual milieu that constrains a writer to avoid the Emperor System [*tennōsei*] as subject matter."[23] Ten years earlier, in the story "Seventeen" and its sequel "A Political Boy Is Now Dead," Ōe had taken up the subject of seventeen-year-old Yamaguchi Otoya, who had assassinated the Socialist Party leader, Asanuma Inejiro, in 1960. These stories caused an uproar. All kinds of political groups, right and left, inundated the author with accusations, protests, and threats. To smooth things over, the publisher, Bungakukai, issued "Our Humble Notice" (*kinkoku*), formally apologizing to the groups involved for the inconveniences the publication incurred, and withdrew the sequel, "A Political Boy Is Now Dead," from publication. The story is still unavailable to the public to this day. This furor was a blessing in disguise. The accusers unwittingly offered the accused a legitimate reason to articulate his position on the Emperor System and its political implications, a position which had continued to fester within him since the midsummer day of August 15, 1945. Politically, things move at a slow pace in "unrevolutionary" Japan, and Ōe let five years pass by before he opened a series of rebuttals to his critics. The message of his argument was disturbingly clear. In 1966, at the August 15 Memorial Meeting, he lashed out in a public lecture at those who refuse to remember the "rare period, the unprecedented time" and "the uninhibited air, the liberated spirit, lodged deep in the hearts of the masses, that made it possible to reexamine the Emperor System inside out."[24] The ideology of the Emperor System is a most effective *kakuremino*, "a magic coat that can make the wearer invisible," he argued, which tells the Japanese "you can quit thinking about the war, you do not have to think about it." Ōe continued: "Those who lost their sons in the war continue to think about the present and prewar Japan, about a possible war in the future. Then let us suppose, at a memorial service of the war dead held somewhere else, the Emperor himself is present." Isn't it just possible, Ōe asked, that the same people, upon learning of the Emperor's attendance, might stop thinking altogether, shed "sweet tears," and start glorifying the war period? (p. 382)

Ōe is unable to accept the memories of the defeat and postwar Japan cherished by the conservatives and their followers, the kind of "cleaned up" memories that have resulted in the elimination of other memories—the newborn, free, critical spirit that permitted the masses for the first time to question the validity of the Emperor System. He argued that "to recall the time" as a period of political liberation is "to violate a taboo. It has become a proscription. . . . I feel what has been suppressing the arts and the minds of the masses of Japan today is nothing other than the Emperor System" (p. 383).

In the month following the public lecture, Ōe again confronted the "intrinsic peculiarity of the Japanese intellectual milieu" that unabashedly buried "A Political Boy" alive. In the article "Can a Writer Remain Absolutely Antipolitical?" he wrote:

> Why is it that those writers who have led such a persistent battle in defense [of a Japanese translation] of *Lady Chatterley's Lover* did not take up the gauntlet for *Fūryūmudan* (Fukazawa Shichiro, 1960) or "Seventeen" [which includes the sequel "A Political Boy Is Now Dead"]? It is because both works concern not so much right-wing elements in Japan as everything that the Emperor System evokes. As a novelist, I did not write "Seventeen" and "A Political Boy Is Now Dead" just for the purpose of studying the rightist movement in Japan. My task was to develop the image I have of the Emperor System and its omnipresence, which penetrates and surrounds our entire being. Probably this was obvious to everyone, and consequently, the author was forced to isolate himself . . . this story ["A Political Boy"] incurred various kinds of political misinterpretations from both conservatives and progressives. I have never, at any point in the story, treated the hero with ridicule. (p. 381)

Ōe quotes two short passages from the ill-fated work, which prefigures the ideology that the thirty-five-year-old narrator in *My Tears* dons as his magic coat:

> The aroma of the tide stiffened my overworked nostrils, sharp and relentless, about to tear them apart. I opened my eyes, took in the sea at dusk lying beyond framed by the window, and shouted, "Oh, your Majesty!"

> I believed I had seen him. I did behold the face of pure white, a light of glittering purple bathing the cheeks, the ears, and the hair, the large ruff with frills of brilliant gold, the scarlet garment donned by those eighteenth-century European kings. The sun going down over the sea is the Emperor himself, the essence of the absolute Emperor like the universe is the sun! Your Majesty, your Majesty, teach me what to do, the minute I prayed from the descending summer sun over the sea I received the revelation. (p. 381)

Trying to commit suicide in solitary confinement, the boy overcomes the fear of death:

> A kind of fearless death, given only to a self-immolating soul, a supreme bliss. His Majesty is the only being that can transcend death, removes the claws of terror from death, transforms terror to supreme bliss. . . . Still unconscious and unborn, I am afloat in the embryonic water, a dark sea of the vast universe, my eyes flooded with a luminescence of gold, rose, and purple. Oh, your Majesty, your Majesty!'' (p. 382)

It is not surprising to see in the image of this rightist boy the ideal youth cherished dearly by Mishima Yukio and canonized a year before his death in the perfect terrorist hero, Isao, in *Runaway Horses* (Honba, 1969). Nor is it surprising to see Ōe's chagrin over the death of Mishima, which he calls ''an intentional effrontery'' and ''an insult'' directed at all the Japanese who have chosen to live through (*ikinobiru*) the postwar years to the present. In ''The Dead: The Ultimate Vision and We Who Continue To Live,'' the last chapter of *The Postwar as the Contemporary* (Dōjidai to shite no sengo), Ōe writes that Mishima, instead of creating a comic novel of black humor and ''grotesque realism,'' justified as an artist the young terrorist's every empty utterance. As a person he rejected criticism by others and rushed into *seppuku* to ''let a flower of destruction bloom just for himself.''[25]

Ōe observes that Mishima's pet theories on ''tradition,'' ''politics,'' and ''the Emperor,'' including his final ''manifesto,'' carefully avoided words, like ''the other,'' ''reality,'' and ''object,'' that would reveal the fragility and contradiction in his argument (p. 294). Such was also the language of literature churned out by the war collaborators. Those ambiguous (*aimaina*) words supported by ''absolute emotions'' fed the military propoganda that led the nation into war. Words that had a mystic spirit constantly sustained the nation and endowed the Emperor with power and wisdom (*kotodama no tasuke tamahau kuni*). The significance of August 15, 1945, is devastating because ''postwar

Japan set out on its troubled journey exempting the cultural tradition headed by the Emperor System from the war responsibilities" (p. 303). The result was that "a dark, huge mass of *resignation*" overshadowed the future of postwar writers.

> However, Mishima was the only postwar writer who had the audacity to reverse the use of this dark, huge mass of *resignation*. He laid his life on the line, guarding the colossal cumulus cloud of the cultural tradition with the Emperor System on top, which was crashing down on postwar writers, as if it were a ray of light in the dark that would illuminate his own "aesthetics." The bewitched "words" of equivocation, "words" created with deliberate ambiguity by his law school mentality and presumptuousness—Mishima uttered the "words," as we have seen in *Runaway Horses*, bedecked with the same ornaments of the fanatical war collaborators. . . .
>
> At this point he publicly insulted all of us who have undertaken the postwar task to build up our literary imagination despite the huge, dark mass of *resignation* watching over us, and those who have tried to follow in our footsteps. . . . And then, as if to dodge the advancing counterattack . . . together with a host of unverifiable "words," he cut his belly open as fireworks of chrysanthemum banged in the sky, as a defender of the cultural tradition whose pinnacle was the Emperor System, of the nation which "the word-soul aids." He had bought and left behind the safest "stock" of a nation, proven with such brutality a quarter century ago, the unyieldingness of its foundation which even the blood deluge of the countless number of war victims could not shake loose. As the flesh of the beautiful, eloquent youth [Isao] substantiated his ultimate vision, Mishima became one with the boy, a red disk of chrysanthemum illuminated his final vision radiantly.[26]

That the death of Mishima galvanized the composition of *My Tears* is no secret. In the prologue of the second publication of *My Tears*, Ōe draws the relationship between Mishima's suicide and the Emperor System: the ostracized "A Political Boy" is still alive and well in Ōe's mind. The devastating reception of the story had led him to seek elsewhere a literary mode that would free him from the "shackles of the Emperor System, a suppressor of political imagination" (p. 245). The most notable thing about Ōe's post-1968 stories that deal with sociopolitical topics is the adoption of black humor, exaggeration, madness, the parodic, and the satiric. *My Tears* maximizes this "legitimacy of the exercise of a free imagination that is politically committed,"[27] but not bound to the mimetic representation of reality. The work is his challenge, as a writer, to "the cultural tradition headed by the Emperor System," whereas Mishima wrote *Runaway Horses* as a justification of that tradition and system. In a world turned upside down, Ōe parodies the "possessed words of equivocation" that allowed Mishima to create the ideal youth, whose eloquent speech is unequalled. The thirty-five-year-old narrator of *My Tears* plays a "double" for both the dead author and the canonized boy, "the wrong side" of everything the Emperor System continues to suggest. Instead of the divine Emperor waiting for the narrator/biographer to wipe his tears away (the title of *My Tears* clearly indicates the presence of the Emperor by the use of the verb "to wipe" in honorific form, *nuguitamō*), it is his mother's "scratchy thumbs" that "expertly wipe away the tears in the corners of his closed eyes."

At the end of a narrative discourse that zigzags, spins, and seesaws, who is given the final words? "Sooner or later the Japanese are going to change their attitude about what happened, and I intend to live to see it, yessir!" (162/105). Such is the hope the narrator's mother expresses. "About what happened" (*kono koto ni tsuite*) refers to August 15, 1945, the one event narrated *n* times in connection with the Emperor System. The mother pities her son for the first time: "And here he is thirty-five years old, it's a cruel business! When he was a child he'd dream the teacher at elementary school was asking him IF THE EMPEROR ORDERED YOU TO DIE, WOULD YOU DIE? and he'd sob and repeat the cruel answer in his sleep, YES, I WOULD DIE, I WOULD DIE HAPPILY! and he is thirty-five years old and still weeping away as if the teacher was asking him that same question, it's a cruel business, yessir!]]" (162–63/105–106). No matter how he shuts himself up in seclusion, whether he is a conservative or a progressive, Ōe repeats, as long as the Emperor System remains, a Japanese writer cannot disavow his political involvement.[28] Writing, for Ōe, is more than "a personal matter": it is a political act.

7

Imagination of Grotesque Realism

In his five works written between 1964 and 1976, Ōe consistently employs the image of a corpulent father and his idiot son setting out on a search for the world of "grotesque realism."[1] These five narratives are "Aghwee the Sky Monster" (Sora no kaibutsu aguwee, 1964, hereafter "Aghwee"), *A Personal Matter* (Kojinteki na taiken, 1964), "Teach Us to Outgrow Our Madness" (hereafter "Teach Us"), *The Waters Are Come in unto My Soul* (Kōzui wa waga tamashii ni oyobi, 1973, hereafter *The Waters*), and *The Pinch-runner Memorandum* (Pinchi rannaa chōsho, 1976, hereafter *The Pinch-runner*). We must not dismiss the presence of this "obsessive metaphor" of the father and the idiot son merely as a repetition of an old theme, but rather must consider the five works as one large narrative in progress. The pertinence of reciprocity between one work and another is well asserted by Todorov: "Just as the meaning of a part of the work is not exhausted in itself, but is revealed in its relation with other parts, a work in its entirety can never be read in a satisfactory and enlightening fashion if we do not put it in relation with other works, previous and contemporary."[2]

To apply Todorov's notion of reciprocity within the works of a single author, we can categorize Ōe's five works into a "syntagmatic" type,[3] in which the second text reacts actively to the first, rather than a paradigmatic type, which indicates the absence of the other text and does not function reciprocally. The first two works, "Aghwee" and *A*

Personal Matter, play off one another, creating the "syntagmatic" or "combinatory" relation between the two represented in the formula of the question/answer pair, or what Todorov calls "a concealed polemic."[4] The main polemic is: "Should I kill the monster baby or live with the monster?" The narrative movement in "Aghwee" is based on the answer, "Yes, I should kill the baby (and I have murdered the baby)." *A Personal Matter* presents the other choice, "No, I should not kill the baby; I will live with the baby." By combining the first text with the second, the reader gains a clearer view of the conflict that the father must have experienced.

Once the resolution to live with the baby is made and the father carries out the decision, there emerges another question/answer: "Am I really the passive victim quietly enduring a bondage imposed by my idiot son who never rejects my words?" This polemic is the basis of the verbal structure of "Teach Us."

Freedom from this artificially created bondage, the father's obsessive desire, means the establishment of a balanced relationship between the father and the son. It also means the exclusion of a mother or a wife, whose original role loses its impetus. To make their life a meaningful one, the pair must have contacts with the external world. Thus *The Waters* and *The Pinch-runner* are adventure stories of the undaunted pair, the former story about the father who assumes the active role in the adventure, the latter about the idiot son who carries out the cosmic vision shared by the father and the son. Both stories end with a death: the father dies in *The Waters*, the son Mori in *The Pinch-runner*. Because Ōe's works are ultimately about Mori the idiot son, Ōe must end his story when the idiot son dies. In the following pages I shall closely examine in sequence the five works about Mori and their "syntagmatic," i.e., "combinatory," relations, which unveil the paradigmatic intertextual figure of the father and the idiot son.

A young father, the main character of "Aghwee," kills his newborn baby by giving him only sugar water. When the autopsy reveals that the baby had a benign tumor, the father goes into self-confinement and becomes obsessed with the illusion (so the narrator and reader are led to believe) of his baby flying down from the sky. The phantom baby, the size of a kangaroo, in a white cotton nightgown dwells in the sky. In other words, the murdered baby is transformed into a celestial being who is part of the cosmic force. According to his ex-wife the father's self-confinement is escapism.

The baby comes down from the sky to remind the father of his crime and taunt him. The illusion/reality perhaps represents the father's insane desire to communicate and join with the baby, whose only utterance in his brief life was "Aghwee!" In the end the baby seems to fulfill the father's desire to join the baby in the sky. Or the narrator speculates that perhaps the baby tricks the father: "Suddenly D [the father] cried out and thrust both arms in front of him as if he were trying to rescue something; then he leaped in among those trucks and was struck to the ground" (152/257–58).[5] In other words, the father lets himself go for the first time in his life and *decides* to follow the baby. Already in this story are mythological elements or elements of the fantastic, which Ōe incorporates into *The Pinch-runner*. The kangaroo baby is not a passive victim eliminated by his own father, but a trickster-like character; he returns to haunt his murderer. The baby character does not exist in reality, but he does exist in the father's psyche. To the narrator, however, hired to be the father's companion, the question persists to the end: does it exist or not?

Seven months after the short story "Aghwee" appeared, Ōe published *A Personal Matter*, which again centers around the father and his idiot son. Antithetical to the previous story, here the newborn baby escapes death by clinging stubbornly to life. Overwhelmed by the infant's physical and instinctive power to survive, the father, called Bird, resolves to live with his idiot son. This yet-to-be named baby serves a double function: he is the cause of the father's personal tragedy as well as a symbol of the tragedy of mankind. For, in the midst of confusion, despair, and enervation, as he is about to murder the baby, Bird hears the news broadcast of the Soviet resumption of nuclear testing. Later he learns that the Japan Anti-Nuclear Warfare League has come out in support of the test: "In a world shared by all those others, time was passing, mankind's one and only time, and a destiny apprehended the world over as one and the same destiny was taking evil shape. Bird, on the other hand, was answerable only to the monster who governed his personal destiny" (355/194).[6]

Sensing the connection between the baby's fate and the fate of mankind, Bird decides to take care of the baby. Bird challenges the odds that are stacked up against him to live with the monster baby, "the creation of misery for himself and the nurturing of a life that meant absolutely nothing to this world." Against these odds he repeats to himself: "It's for my own good. It's so I can stop being a man who's always running away. . . ." "All I want is to stop being a man who continually runs away from responsibility" (367/211). Here, Ōe's hero reverses his relation to reality and to the world. Instead of saying, "What is wrong with me? What have I done to deserve this tragedy?" he begins to act upon reality by asking, "What is my meaningful relation to the world?" Ōe shares the Dostoevskian view that the most important thing is "not how the hero appears to the world, but . . . how the world appears to the hero and how the hero appears to himself."[7]

Thus the baby is the beginning of the father's new life, a life of commitment to the world. We see in the three subsequent stories, "Teach Us," *The Waters,* and *The Pinch-runner,* how the odds are turned around, how the existence of an idiot son becomes part and parcel of the father's entire being. The identification of the father with the infant son gradually takes place at the end of *A Personal Matter*: "A week after the operation the baby had looked almost human; the following week it had begun to resemble Bird" (368/212). Also, the final paragraph implies that the father is slowly emerging from an amorphous, suspended existence (*chūburarinko*), about to embark upon a risky adventure in the world where idiocy is an anomaly, a digression from the norms set up by the intolerant society. The baby's presence will eventually liberate the father from the self-indulgence he has allowed. Ōe's works seek to explore "the sum total" of the hero's (later the pair's—the father and the idiot son's) "consciousness and self-consciousness . . . the hero's final word about himself and about his world."[8]

In "Teach Us" Ōe strikes upon a name most appropriate for the idiot son, a name which allegorically unites Ōe to the environment he himself grew up in, a valley in the deep forest of Shikoku Island (the background of "Prize Stock," 1957). Mori, "forest" in Japanese and "death or idiocy" in Latin, becomes the axis upon which Ōe's literary universe spins and expands. At the same time Mori is also the destination to which Ōe returns. The father initially meant to mock his son whose alternative was to die or be an idiot. "Could such existence be given a name?"(55/176).[9] "Mori!—Every time he called the child by name it seemed to him he could hear, in the profound darkness in his head, his own lewd and repentent laughter mocking the entirety of his life" (55/177). His cynicism turns against him, and he is the one to be mocked.

The corpulent father identifies with the moon-faced four-year-old son and tries to live in his son's twilight world filled with pain, fear, and numbness. He believes or wants to believe that he is the only one who can function as a window to his son's murky mind, as "a pipeline of vision connecting his son's brain" with the outside world through the "conduit of their clasped hands." However, an incident occurs that forces the father to realize his son's adaptability: "My son can get along without me, as an idiot in an idiot's way. . ." (81/212). The situation reverses: the fat man, believing that he has brought order, peace, and harmony to his son's fragile existence, must accept the truth. It is the father who depends upon his son for assurance, comfort, and equilibrium. Throughout the story the reader is made familiar with the fat son not by his real name, Mori, but by his nickname, Eeyore, which, according to the Japanese pronunciation, sounds like "*iiyō*," meaning "it's O.K."!

"Teach Us" tells of the initiation of a young father into the outside world filled with terror, pain, and numbness. It is also a story of a father yearning to go back to his childhood and to speak to his own father, who continually ignored him. To the fat man, his own father's strange self-confinement in the darkness of a storehouse, his corpulence, silence, and sudden death are as much a mystery as the idiocy of his infant son. The desire to establish an intimacy, "the heavy bond of restraints," between himself and Mori betrays a chokingly painful question he dares not utter: "Why was my son born an idiot? Is this monster my creation?" In trying to answer this question, the fat man digs a mine in order to reach the core of the pain, and of primeval existence, at the center of which stands Mori.

The father's quest must continue as he experiences Mori's growth. The Mori character is named Jin in *The Waters*, a two-volume novel published in 1973.[10] As if to make up for the poor eyesight the four-year-old Mori had to put up with, Jin, at the age of five, exhibits an extremely keen sense of sound. All day long, he listens to and identifies the songs of wild birds and whales recorded on tape by his father. In flashbacks we learn about Jin's self-destructive impulses and the self-inflicted pain from which he was never free. Just as Mori's father began to feel the pains his son received from a scalding or an eye examination (which terrified Mori), Jin's father develops sudden fainting spells or experiences a scorching pain. Out of desperation, his wife agrees to let the pair of misfits start a new life on their own, a life of tranquility in a refurbished nuclear bomb shelter, totally secluded from the humdrum of the external world.

The name Ōki Isana, which the father takes for himself upon venturing into a new life with Jin, literally means Mr. Brave-Fish Big-Tree. Ōe's choice of this humorous name makes the comic function of the father and son pair evident. The father, claiming to be the agent for the souls of trees and whales, which he believes are the legitimate owners of the earth, exchanges telepathic communications with their spirits. When the entire human population is wiped out by nuclear war, he believes, he will emerge out of the bomb shelter with Jin and return the earth to the trees and whales.

In *The Waters* Ōe again takes up the image of misfits that dominated his early works. For the first time he unites social outcasts, marginals, who heretofore struggled separately, to form a collective body to resist those who stigmatize them as "social cancer." It is significant that dropout characters calling themselves "Freedom Voyagers" form a comradeship with the father and Jin. The nonconformists consist of high school dropouts, ex-college students, a middle-aged Hiroshima survivor called "the Shrinking Man," and the only female member, Inako, who recruits a Self-Defense Corps member by sexual persuasion.

Through Isana's involvement with the "Freedom Voyagers," Jin for the first time encounters a female outsider who respects his idiocy and takes care of him. At first sight Inako (a pun on "grasshoppers," *inago*) is immediately captivated by the infant's innocence, quiet voice, and warm smile. As Jin's "surrogate mother," Inako helps him experience physical contact with others. One day, Isana learns how Inako has succeeded in communicating with Jin:

> What the wench [*komusume*] was doing was to play the tape forward little by little, stop it abruptly, and replay it. Ready to cover his ears with his hands in anticipation that Jin would soon start screaming, Isana was going to climb up the ladder to interfere with Inako, who probably had no idea why she suddenly began to do something so cruel. However, it seemed that some sort of game was in progress between the young woman and the infant, who were sitting on the floor against the couch. Jin was neither frightened nor angry, but looked lively and thoughtful, participating in a game with a stranger for the first time in his life. The woman played the tape forward, a wild bird chirped, and she stopped the tape sharply.
>
> ——It is a Japanese Jungle Nightjar, Jin responded.
> A second passed.
> ——Jin, you made it, a Japanese Jungle Nightjar, a bull's eye! the woman said. The reason she let a second pass was that she was consulting the record jacket which had the names of the wild birds which Isana recorded on tape.[11] (98–99)

An ex-employee of a big corporation and son-in-law of a powerful conservative politician, Ōki Isana shares the lot of the nonrevolutionary "Freedom Voyagers" and dies fighting for a vision, for the "goodness" of the earth, that is, the souls of trees and whales. What is amiss in the farcical repartee between the voyagers awaiting the final assault in the bomb shelter and a police riot squad surrounding the shelter is the voice of Jin the idiot son, who has already been removed from the battle scene by the protective Inako. What the reader and the father want to hear is Jin's soft-spoken voice intoning the words, "The end of the world is here," the Day of Judgment. Jin seems to be a voiceless prophet, calling the world to repentance, representing mankind about to be annihilated by nuclear war.

The father constantly thinks about this role his son is to play at the end of the world. During one of the "bus trips" to the "outside" world, as he holds Jin with one arm, Isana cranes his neck frantically to look at their home, the bomb shelter, which is fast disappearing from his sight. The omniscient narrator tells us:

> Why did he physically have to ascertain the position of the shelter? It was because, at the outbreak of a global nuclear war, Jin and he would have to walk back to the shelter pushing their way through the citizens who had fallen into total panic, with the coolness and tenacity of people who had prepared themselves all their lives for that day, before the heat of the nuclear explosion and shock waves would reach the city. Until that very moment when he and the infant were to return the earth to the trees and whales, they would have to sit back and wait as if willingly accepting the end of mankind. Once the outside concrete walls of the shelter were exposed to the scorching heat, the shock waves would surely reach the ears of the infant. At that instant, Isana hoped he would hear Jin's calm, whispering voice,
> ——The end of the world is here. (22)

In Isana's private world, Jin also provides him with a sense of comfort and security. He is the very meaning of the father's life.

> Sensing that Jin was about to wake up, he [Isana] peered down from the bed. He took pains to determine the proper angle of his body which would make the lighting in the room shine on both his face and the infant's, and help them acknowledge each other's presence. The infant woke up normally. In the good eye and even in the bad one which had poor vision, there was a generous expression of joy that recognized his own father. Around the eyelashes, from which emanated the iridescent luster of an

oyster shell, he flickered a faint, mature smile and identified the bird on the tape,

——It is a Temminick's Crowned Willow-Warbler, and gave a fragrant, small yawn.

An incredible joy bubbled up in Isana's body. (32–33).

Whenever Jin hears a chirping outside, he is capable of identifying the bird and lets Isana know "in a soft voice as imperceptible as breathing itself" (50). In the father's painstaking efforts to carry on "conversations" with Jin, he repeats his speech over and over again until Jin automatically parrots it: "——Let's cook spaghetti noodles, and I'll tell you what happened to me today," he repeated again and again and did not give up until the infant finally responded, ——We'll cook spaghetti noodles, and I'll tell you" (33). Here Ōe seems to be satirizing the sanctity of words and of human communication via words, i.e., the function of *parole* ("actual speech").[12] The failure of communication between the father and the idiot son, represented by the absence of speech, or of the reciprocity of words and ideas, transforms itself into comical dialogues that dominate the narrative flow in both *The Waters* and *The Pinch-runner*. Divested of human deception, false seriousness, and manipulation, the father and his "parroting" son perform something other than what verbal communication can provide.

The Pinch-runner combines three dominant themes with which Ōe has insistently dealt for two decades: the embattlement of marginals, idiocy, and averbalization, and the annihilation of the human race by nuclear war. *The Pinch-runner* is the story of a former nuclear engineer, a thirty-eight-year-old father who has an eight-year-old idiot son, Mori. This undaunted pair goes through a "miraculous transformation": Mori gains twenty years and his father loses twenty. The grown-up Mori "speaks" in the voice of the Cosmic Will and transmits the message to the teenage father through the conduit of their clasped hands. Together they go out, aided by their faithful comrades and the Yamame Army, to eliminate the Patron ("The Big Shot A") of the underworld, who secretly plans to control Japan by financing the manufacture of atomic bombs by two radical groups.

Two central themes posited in the novel need to be scrutinized carefully for us to grasp Ōe's semantic universe as a totality and a dynamic unity. The first is the theme of the "transformation" (*tenkan*), literally, "switch-over," or "metamorphosis," an essential element of fantastic literature.[13] The second is the function of language and the speech act (verbalization) in relation to Mori, the idiot son.

The two themes are not as incompatible or incongruous as they seem. The fantastic universe, based on the exclusion of "luck" or "chance," operates on the principle of "pan-determinism." This principle signifies that "the limit between the physical and the mental, between matter and spirit, between word and thing, ceases to be impervious." In this sense, the notion of metamorphosis or transformation, which "constitutes a transgression of the separation between matter and mind as it is generally conceived," is permissable.[14]

Coeval with the fantastic universe is the world of drugs, the mystic, the psychotic, and, what is most relevant to our discussion, the primordial world of infancy. What characterizes the being of an infant is the effacement of the limit between subject and object, of the normal barrier between the self and the world (the other). To go a step further, his universe is a world without language. Such is the cosmic fusion that the transformed pair, Mori and his father, continuously approaches.

Like madness, Mori's idiocy is in effect a deviation from the norms set up by society or the "natural" world in which ordinary events occur; it is also a transgression of the laws of nature. Therefore, the only way Mori is allowed to exist is to become part of the universe of the fantastic. While the reader experiences a "hesitation" in the face of an apparently supernatural event, Mori's (the father's) miraculous transformation, he can accept Mori because the transformation occurs in the context of natural, everyday life.

The central trait of the fantastic is ambiguity. "The fantastic confronts us with a dilemma: to believe or not to believe."[15] This element of ambiguity is maintained throughout *The Pinch-runner*. First, the separation of the narrator (Mori's father) and his ghost writer (the father of another retarded son, Hikari), who receives the former's utterances through telephone calls, cassette tapes, and letters and writes them down, is purposely weakened from the very beginning of the story. The concept of "double," the fusion of "I-Thou," is described in the first sentence of the novel:

> Words uttered by another party—there was no mistake about it: despite my distinct memory of the circumstance under which the other made the utterance, it was as if these selfsame words gushed out of the deepest recesses of my own soul.[16] (7)

Ōe also stresses the fact that these two fathers have a lot in common and form a complementary relationship. Mori's father and Hikari's father are both of the same generation and are both graduates of Tokyo

University, the former with a science degree (nuclear physics) and the latter with a philosophy degree (literature). They both have idiot sons of the same age. Their initial encounter takes place on the playground where they wait absent-mindedly for "their children" to finish their special class while watching the "brainy children different from theirs" noiselessly play baseball. Reminiscing about the sandlot baseball era he was brought up in, Mori's father mumbles to himself: "Nothing was quite as petrifying, soul-stirring, as being picked as a pinch-runner!" (7). Immediately something inexplicable unites the two men. "At the same instant, . . . a hot, cumbersome, twisted cord, like the *bond* of parent and child, not as simple as anything like symphathy, ran between us" (7). The "I-thou" fusion of the two fathers foreshadows the ambiguous world of the fantastic.

By the end of the first chapter we are prepared for the supernatural event to come, or, to be more exact, for the supernatural event that has already occurred but has not yet been reported. Then, the first narrator of the novel (Hikari's father) is replaced by Mori's father (referred to as "the other party"), who recounts the supernatural event that has overtaken him and his idiot son.

From the second chapter on, the relation between Mori's father and Hikari's father becomes that of "the person who emits the text and the person who receives."[17] Ōe's narrative complicates this verbal structure even more by making the receiver of codes a ghost writer whose main job is to record the utterances or the speech act of Mori's father, not to decode them. We read at the beginning of the story the ghost writer's feeble claim that he is an independent entity and deserves to be treated as such: "Although my job originates in the words of the other party, the words must go through my flesh and consciousness before they can be put down on paper. I'm expected to enter the mind of Mori's father, learn in detail his secret, and even temporarily must grasp the entirety of his being. However, I refuse to accept the reversal of this; I resent his constant habitation in my world" (40).

What sustains the narrative construction of the supernatural event is the tripartite bond that unites the narrator (Mori's father), the chronicler (Hikari's father), and the reader, who is sandwiched between the two.[18] The narrator occasionally questions the ghost writer, "Do you doubt my words? I want you to write in such a way that your faltering voice would merge with my insistent voice of self-assertion and the two voices, one on top of the other, resonate together. The verbal account must be sustained by the tense opposition of my insistent words to your silent misgivings'' (109). The ambiguity caused by Mori's father's use of a ''ghost writer'' makes the reader hesitate because the distinction between the narrator and the receiver of codes gradually ceases. The consciousness of the former begins to envelop the mental activities of the other. As the word indicates, although a ghost writer physically exists, he has no claim to the work he is ''writing.'' Conversely, since the real writer has nothing to do with the actual recording of his words, how can the reader really know that the utterance or the text is actually produced by the professed writer, and not by his ghost writer?

Mori's father gives the following reason why he is asking (actually imposing upon) Hikari's father, whose profession is ''writing,'' to become his scribe:

> Because I need someone to recognize my actions and thoughts, to record them beforehand in a ''memorandum.'' I'm about to embark upon a new adventure with Mori; without the existence of a chronicler, I feel the adventure-to-come, Mori and me, will be merely a maddening illusion. I have a premonition that our adventure will be a fantastic event; if my ''memorandum'' ever ends up in the hands of the police, they would simply dismiss it as balderdash, you know. (38)

On the syntactic level, the novel is a ''game'' about the narrator's gamble: on which side will the reader be? Will he believe the narrator's words or side with the faltering voice of the chronicler?

Ōe links this hesitation, a dilemma whether to believe or not to believe, with the father's fear and intense desire to be selected as a ''pinch-runner.'' His main job is to steal a base and run: the crowd urges him to run. If he miscalculates in the situation, he loses and will be ordered back to sit on the bench. If he wins, he will become, even if temporarily, a hero. His choice is, ''Should I stay or run?'' The grown-up Mori says once via telepathy: ''If the transformation means that we've got to run, as a pinch-runner, for those who can't run, or for those who don't know they must run, then we've got to start running any minute now'' (127). The father/narrator must face this verbal choice, ''Should I stay or run?'' again and again. ''I heard the voices of the spectators urging me to run, after an unexpected hit-and-run came about'' (159–60). In the end this verbal choice becomes the message of the story, the purpose of the adventure of the transformed pair, Mori and the father: ''I was resolved to assert my conviction that we're the chosen ones to run as a pinch-runner for mankind. . . . We've already been selected and sent to the base with the instructions given to us by the coach of the Cosmic Will; we must concentrate our minds on whether we should stand by cautiously or run. However, we must rely on our intuition in the end and must run on our own accord'' (262).

What the narrator anticipates eagerly from the fantastic event, i.e., the transformation, is to see his and Mori's consciousness expand and their flesh renewed and rejuvenated, which he believes is the fundamental hope cherished by the whole of humanity. To renew one's consciousness and flesh, old tissue and the entire past must die, because "renewal" must replace "death." The reversal of time is the key in fantastic literature. That is why the eight-year-old Mori, whose mental universe is that of an infant or a madman, sheds his old infant self and becomes an "adult simulacrum of infancy"[19] in a world without language. On the other hand, Mori's father steadily regresses and becomes "Mori's son," with the possibility of reverting back to infancy.

In recounting this supernatural event, Mori's father suffers from a terrible suspicion that gnaws at him. Isn't our transformation a terrible mistake? What is it that we are entrusted with by the Cosmic Will? Do we really have a mission to carry out? At one point, he begins to doubt the existence of the Cosmic Will, and instead begins to believe that the political domination of the Patron might be the very cause of their transformation. What pulls him out of this deep skepticism is Mori: at the age of twenty-eight, with his quiet smile, animated eyes, and silence, he communicates with his teenage father. The narrator tells the chronicler: "This transformed Mori is the real Mori, the ultimate Mori, the beginning of Mori. So long as this Mori exists in reality, I will live through the life of 'transformation' with him, and carry out the job entrusted to us by the Cosmic Will'' (85).

The dreams and the imaginary/the illusory scattered throughout the verbal account indicate "the ambiguous vision" of the narrator that relies on the use of the stylistic device of modalization.[20] Thus, the narrator talks of a possibility (and a hope) of one day decoding what must be stored in Mori's dark, murky brain: "As in a sealed cell, where dust *must* eventually accumulate over a long period of time, my words, the fine particles of dust, *might* one day form a heap and by natural ignition start into flame. At least Mori never rejects my words. Who knows, deep in the dim cell of Mori's twilight brain, the words transmitted to him through the eardrum *might* have been stored away like the sand in an hourglass'' (43).

At one point, the father imagines that Mori is a Socrates: "Listening quietly with genuine interest to whatever I tell him, Mori must be a man like Socrates who awakens you to your ignorance and raises you to a new level of knowledge'' (93). In the mind of the narrator, dream and reality, or the imaginary and the real, do not form separate and impermeable blocks. Time and again, Mori's father sees a dream of an extraordinary event that foretells their future: one such dream is about the Patron whom the pair helps gain total political power in Japan, power that extends to Korea, and the pageant they direct to celebrate his victory. However, the festival immediately turns itself into a celebration of the death of the Patron. The pair has rebelled against him and succeeds in the elimination of the evil force.

In the dream of the "Long March," Mori and the father are members of the Yamame Army which has in reality rescued the pair from the violent mob who refused to listen to Mori's message transmitted from the Cosmic Will. The pair is now a part of the collective body of "ideal people." The father recognizes among the Yamame soldiers those friends he encountered in his life. These are the people who have given him "a sense of fullness, stability, and finally the liberation of his soul" (235). Passing right before him, accompanied by his lovely French wife, is a dear friend of his who strangled himself in Paris. In reality he was the Yamame Army agent based in Europe. Gijin, the leader of the antinuclear movement from Shikoku, is also in the march, "walking stiffly like a toy soldier with his hands clasped tight on his chest" (236), as though he had been resurrected from death. The father's idol, Ōno Sakurao, walks right beside him. Hikari and his father complete the list of comrades who join the Long March. The narrator tells the scribe, "After all, I've been telling a dream-like dream all along, ha ha!" (234).

Dreams or the imaginary in the novel have a double function. One is vaticinal in the sense that they are the harbingers of things to come; the other is to remove the boundaries between matter and spirit, the physical and the mental. What happens throughout the story is the materialization of the imaginary and the perceived. The entire verbal account, based on the sender of codes (narrator) and the receiver of codes (ghost writer), is turned upside down. The reader is uncertain whether the narrator and the ghost writer are really two separate people, or whether the entire verbal act originates in the real, rather than in the imaginary/the illusory, or "a dream-like dream."

This ambiguity or hesitation is not cleared away at the end of the novel. The narrator's "alternate plan" in case of his or Mori's death or arrest is revealed to the ghost writer, who is to substitute as the sender of codes to recount the end of their adventurous journey. We must assume that that is exactly what happens, and that the obstacle between the person who produces the text and the person who receives it collapses.

*   *   *

The aesthetic concept governing *The Pinch-runner* comes from what Bakhtin defines as "grotesque realism" in his discussions of *Gargantua and Pantagruel*.[21] In grotesque realism the bodily functions are always affirmed in an "all-popular," festive, utopian setting. The cosmic, social, and bodily elements are parts of an indivisible whole and are presented not in a private, egotistical form or isolated from the other aspects of life, but as something universal, representing all people. The other side of the essential principle of grotesque realism is "degradation, that is, the lowering of all that is high, spiritual, ideal, abstract; it is a transfer to the material level, to the sphere of earth and body in their indissoluble unity" (pp. 19–20).

Rabelais challenged the authority of the still-medieval Church which inculcated fear and blind obedience in the minds of individuals. For this "battle," the great French satirist armed himself with a panoply of pots, frying pans, chopping knives, and with the urine and excrement of Gargantua and Pantagruel, which destroy yet fertilize the earth. Rabelais also knew that his criticism of the authority of Catholicism was deadly because he was an insider who was constantly exposed to the hypocrisy of clerical power. What he attempted to do was to turn the world and the conventional worldview upside down by demystifying "upward is heaven, downward is earth." According to Bakhtin, "Earth is an element that devours, swallows up (the grave, the womb) and at the same time an element of birth, or renascence (maternal breasts). Such is the meaning of 'upward' and 'downward' in their cosmic aspect, while in their purely bodily aspect, which is not clearly distinct from the cosmic, the upper part is the face or the head and the lower part is the genital organs, the belly, the buttocks" (p. 21).

Bakhtin's analysis sheds light on Ōe's constant reference to the lower part of the human body or bodily elements and copulation. The eight-year-old Mori, whose entire being exists in the need to eat, urinate, defecate, and sleep, is, in the world of groteque realism, not an imbecile but a positive being. He is acceptable in this world because he embodies the principle of degradation and debasement, which draws upon the excessive, the ludicrous, the exaggerated, and the earthy. For example, at night Mori must still wear a diaper though it is no longer big enough to cover his growing buttocks and erect penis. When we read the passage that describes Mori splashing urine all over the restroom, unable to aim his penis properly into the toilet, we do not find him pathetic, but laughable. Laughter degrades and yet materializes, writes Bakhtin. Degradation "has not only a destructive, negative aspect, but also a regenerating one." To degrade an object or a person implies hurling it or him down to "the zone in which conception of a new birth takes place" (p. 21).

Laughter in groteque realism is shared by all people; it is a festive laughter that removes the barrier of human prejudice and deception, where "all men become conscious participants in that one world of laughter" (p. 188). It heals and regenerates. "Laughter must liberate the gay truth of the world from the veils of gloomy lies spun by the seriousness of fear, suffering, and violence" (p. 174). Although man is the only living creature endowed with laughter, when we think of laughter in the context of modern Japanese literature, we are struck by its poverty. It seems that laughter is "an ostracized slut" and has never been fully recognized as a proper ingredient for a novel. Laughter is born out of the masses, the uneducated, common ordinary people. It is the vulgar, simplistic, popular nature that is inherent in laughter. In other words, by its very association with common folk, laughter has always occupied a "debased" position and has been considered something frivolous and trivial. Particularly in the early days of the rise of the modern novel (1868–1925), when Japanese intellectuals were busily engaged in soul searching or in carrying out their visionary mission, laughter rarely was a source of inspiration and creativity.[22]

In contrast to the vision pursued by the Meiji-Taishō intellectuals, Ōe's private quest and literary world constantly draw upon the festiveness and universality of laughter. Farcical slapstick and travesty abound in *The Pinch-runner*. Or, to put it another way, those incidents that we consider serious and earthshaking in the context of ordinary life are debased and lowered down to the bodily elements of the earth. Nothing is vulgar in Ōe's universe: everything is told matter-of-factly in its utopian, all-popular organic wholeness.

For example, the novel describes a type of meeting (*hanseikai*) familiar to all Japanese. It is designed to "reflect upon" a past event in order to improve the situation, in the manner of a roundtable discussion. A *hanseikai* is held to thank Mori's father for rescuing one of the children who gets caught in the malfunctioning automatic door of a supermarket where the whole "special class" has gone shopping. With the principal and the two embarrassed teachers in front of him, Mori's father goes into an eloquent tirade, trying to reevaluate and reform the entire system of the Special School and the function of the teachers who work under the system.

> The only real help you can give *our children* is to tell them what the contemporary world's really like out there, what they should keep an eye out for! That's what you should be telling them. Is it possible at all? Are you really teaching *our children* what they need? All you're doing is teaching them how to take care of their arms and legs so that in the future they can at least live independently as imbeciles. . . . Who knows, this system might accommodate itself . . . isn't it possible that *our children* might end up studying how to dispose of not only their arms and legs but the whole body, in other words, ha, ha, how to commit suicide? . . . We must teach them how to take up arms and defend themselves, to drive back this authoritarian force which would weed them out of the future society. As long as this world continues to be contaminated, the population of those like *our children* will skyrocket. . . . They'll one day be marked as the object of hatred for the masses, a symbol of the downbeat society to come. (34)

The principal, replying to Mori's father's radical suggestion, upholds the status quo: "As a specialist in physical education, it has been my belief that education means to teach the unity of mind and spirit, and how to reconcile oneself with nature and society" (34). This is a hackneyed statement repeated again and again to students in secondary education, and Mori's father is perfectly aware of the conventionality of the principal's response. Mori's father immediately offers an alternative, which is to teach the children music. "Since all of *our children* have good ears, we'll make them specialists in music" (35). He solemnly starts reading the memoirs on a record jacket written by a guru of Indian music. The reading session and meditation abruptly come to an end when the widow mother of Saachan protests loudly.

> ——*WHAT THE HELL IS A GURU*!? What the hell do you mean by India? . . . By a raga? You talk these kids blind with bullshit; they're perfectly still, not understanding a word, exhausted and hungry. *WHAT THE HELL ARE YOU, WHAT, WHAT!?* YOU . . .
>   . . .
> ——When we held meetings, to get rid of the discrimination that shuts

up *our children* in the special class, you showed up only once; we thought we could count on you, but you never came back! *WHAT THE HELL ARE YOU TALKING ABOUT!?* You say we make *our children* music special-ists? How about a kid like Saachan who's hard of hearing? Do you mean to say we're going to discriminate against her even in the special class? No more discrimination! Pray for your guru, guru, so that you won't make a mistake! Feel up the bountifulness of the T.V. personality's ass! You sexual pervert! (36)

The meeting deteriorates and turns into a shouting match between the mother and a woman teacher, who tries to quiet her. The parents busily take care of their children who need to urinate, or clean up the urine and feces of those children who could not hold out. In the midst of this commotion sits Mori, quietly wetting himself.

What is at work in the comical, farcical descriptions that abound in *The Pinch-runner* is travesty combined with cartoon or cartoonized travesty. Ōe is an inveterate cartoonist; as a cartoonist he is also very much aware of the power of satire, which responds to "the world with a mixture of laughter and indignation."[23] In this sense, festive laughter, which destroys the clerical authority during the "feast of fools" and the "feast of the ass" in the Middle Ages,[24] and the way of satire, which turns the real world upside down, share much. Both grotesque realism and satire involve "a cathartic release of social tension."[25] Rabelaisian laughter and satire complement each other in aiding us to unveil the constituents of Ōe's semantic world: "True satire demands a high degree both of commitment to and involvement with the painful prob-lems of the world, and simultaneously a high degree of abstraction from the world. The criticism of the world is abstracted from its ordinary setting, . . . political oratory and journalism, and transformed into a high form of 'play'; which gives us both the recognition of our respon-sibilities and irresponsible joy of make-believe."[26]

In the "workshop" episode —shopping at a supermarket—followed by the self-abortive *hanseikai*, Ōe treats an extremely serious and delicate subject that directly concerns his personal life and the lives of those parents who have retarded children. The more serious the subject matter, however, the more he intentionally relaxes concern by exhibiting the dramatic process of the episode as ludicrous, because comedy is "most effectively comic when it treats of things which do arouse our concern."[27] According to Ōe, there is always a serious element in buffoonery and cartoonization, and the ludicrous is seen only in comparison with the conventional.

The whole episode relies on the principle that the reader's only natural physical response to the pathetic handicapped children is laughter, and that this is directed neither at the children nor at their defensive parents. What is being laughed at is the overall action, or the process that reveals the inadequate system of the Special School and its incompetent servants (the principal and the two teachers), who adamantly adhere to the status quo. The principal, a physical education major whose philosophy lies in the unification of mind and spirit, the reconciliation of society and nature, becomes the object of laughter.[28] His comment has absolutely no value for the education of retarded children. Furthermore, he is just a paper pusher and has no interest in special education. In the end he takes advantage of the unexpected turn of events and slips out of the room, "like a monkey," while the widow mother continues to bark up the wrong tree.

This incident contains, as in the case of all good satire, "an element of aggressive attack and a fantastic vision of the world transformed."[29] What sets it off from conventional satire, however, is the absence of contemptuous laughter or a bitter aftertaste. The overall spirit of satire is taken over by festive laughter, which degrades and regenerates.

Another sociopolitical incident, nuclear hijacking, also becomes the object of satire and Rabelaisian laughter in *The Pinch-runner*. It happens when the father is working as an engineer for a nuclear power plant (I call him the father here, even though the incident occurs prior to the birth of Mori, because the narrator has given him no other name besides Mori-chichi, "Mori–father.") At one point in the story the father accompanies a driver and his assistant in broad daylight, completely unarmed and unguarded, hauling enough nuclear material to produce twenty A-bombs. A small, old-fashioned truck with a tarpaulin forces the power plant truck to halt. Jumping out from under the tarpaulin are five or six men garbed like the "Tin Man" in *The Wizard of Oz*, each carrying a pitchfork (*sasumata*). When the father recognizes that the tin men's small truck is also used to deliver school lunches, his mind is seized with the fear and excitement he experienced as a pinch-runner in a sandlot baseball game when he was a boy. "How intoxicating, petrifying, it was to be picked as a pinch-runner!" And he continues, "Once they load the truck with the plutonic acid and reuse the vehicle for delivering school luncheons in Tokyo, contamination will spread among the schoolchildren!" (62). He makes up his mind to "run and steal the base" and jumps under the tarpaulin, squatting down among barrels that contain the radiated green liquid. One of the barrels breaks open as the tin men prod the father with pitchforks, at which point he goes berserk and starts screaming wildly. "Everything's contaminated! Everything, the truck, the driveway, all of us! Alert! Alert!" (62). He keeps on screaming until the tin men start fleeing from the scene, making terrible clink-clank noises in their cumbersome costumes.

In this episode the gravity of the situation—the astronomical risk taken by handling plutonium and possessing nuclear power, and the possibility of radiation contamination—is debased to the level of comical combat between the hijackers and the hijacked. No Geiger counter, armed guards, or terrorism are involved. Things are turned around: the hijacked psychologically terrorizes the hijackers.

In another episode, the transformed pair, the teenage father and the grown-up Mori, attend an antinuclear meeting organized by a television personality, Ōno Sakurao, and the Revolutionary Party. Above the stage set up by Ōno Sakurao is a banner, "Nuclear Power in the Hands of Non-Authority." Beethoven's string quartet "Serioso," Op. 95, plays in the background and intoxicates the whole audience. Mori's father, whose sexual prowess has been restored to that of an eighteen-year-old, is constantly aroused by the sight of his idol, Ōno Sakurao, on the stage. Also at the meeting are Mori and Mori's activist girlfriend, Sayoko; the leader of the antinuclear forces on Shikoku Island, Gijin; and the Volunteer Mediator (*Shigan Chūsainin*), who constantly gets himself into trouble by trying to mediate the conflict between the two factions within the antinuclear forces, the Revolutionary Party and the Counter-Revolutionary Party.

The members of the Counter-Revolutionary Party who have infiltrated the audience start disrupting the meeting. The solemn political gathering, interrupted by a short-circuit in the lighting system, degenerates into a commotion, and the commotion into a riot in which young activists of the Revolutionary Party start punching each other on the stage in the semidarkness of disco-like flashing lights. The riot becomes a free-for-all, and the distinction between friend and foe is totally lost. Right below the stage Gijin bites the assailants using his only weapon, his false teeth, which have been knocked out of his mouth, as pincers. The Volunteer Mediator confronts the physical violence with his undaunted spirit, tenacity, and flexibility. On the stage, the mob, jostling, pushing, beating each other up, gleefully throws the television star into the air. What catches the eyes of the teenage father "in heat" is his beloved, above the bobbing heads of the activists, struggling helter-skelter, trying to kick her way out. The valiant teenager rescues his "princess" and both retreat to a switchboard room backstage while the riot squad breaks into the meeting hall, "like tidal waves," and takes control. Mori's father assures Ōno Sakurao, "The riot squad won't dare come into this room with their metallic shields!" (104). While he experiences "a fantastic orgasm" in making love to her, everything quiets down outside: the two take leave of the switchboard room with a flashlight which illuminates a big sign with a skull and crossbones, "KEEP OUT. HIGH VOLTAGE." Here we see the comical turn of events, copulation in the face of death, the antinuclear forces torn apart by factionalism.

All the various elements of grotesque realism are brought together in the eleventh chapter of *The Pinch-runner*, "The Arrival of the Buffoons." Fifty people who come from the Patron's district congregate outside the hospital to exorcise the evil spirits for their dying Patron. The country people throng around the building in pairs, disguised as *yakuza* (Japanese mafia), folk heroes, the Marx Brothers, Chaplin, A-bomb victims, *kamikaze* pilots, etc.

The carnivalesque, all-popular, cosmic world is recreated in the gathering of these fifty buffoons. The father ruminates upon sighting a pair of buffoons, a dwarf and his companion, an outlandishly corpulent woman: "Their very physical handicap satisfies the conditions of buffoonery, which is the degradation and debasement of the standard" (62). For the first time, the idiot son Mori and the father have found a crowd in which they fit comfortably. The transformed pair joins the pressing throng in costumes that accentuate their transformation. Mori's father, in a rabbit-ear baby suit "as big as a kangaroo," moves steadily toward infancy, and Mori, in the costume of a wizard, approaches senility.

The Patron, who is in reality a terrifying authority figure, becomes the clown to be mocked in this carnivalesque world: the buffoons are there to uncrown the dying "king," to let a new "king" reign. In other words, the only way the fifty country folk can overcome their fear of authority is to disguise themselves as buffoons, because only buffoonery, under the influence of a masquerade atmosphere, can summon the power of another world, a new world, a new ruler. We see here Ōe's attempt to "indigenize" (*dochakuka*) buffoonery and the carnival, which have always existed as "little traditions" in the villages but have been forgotten: "In an era in which the exterior of a city like Tokyo seems to have been buried under the debris of modernization, and where the idea of buffoonery seems virtually dead, subterranean society, like the world of the rain trout (*iwana*),[30] can still offer us a place for the birth, growth, and death of buffoonery" (244).

As Ōe discusses in detail in "Toward the Imagination of Buffoonery and Regeneration," the image of a buffoon is closely related to the mythological figure of the trickster, "The Foolish One." The trickster is "a breaker of the holy taboos, a destroyer of the most sacred objects," yet, to the Winnebago Indians, he is "a positive force, a builder." What takes place in the figure of the trickster is the gradual evolution "from an amorphous, instinctual, unintegrated being into one with the lineaments of man and one foreshadowing man's psychical traits."[31] He is "at one and the same time creator and destroyer, giver and negator, he who dupes others and who is always duped himself. He wills nothing consciously. At all times he is constrained to behave as he does from impulses over which he has no control. He knows neither good nor evil yet he is responsible for both. He possesses no values, moral or social, is at the mercy of his passions and appetites, yet through his actions all values come into being."[32] The trickster figure is an archetype of the jester and the buffoon, the ancestor of a Rabelaisian hero. One essential trait that characterizes the trickster, a creature still living in his unconscious with the mentality of a child, is ambivalence. In this sense the idiot son Mori becomes Ōe's trickster. For example, as a small child, terrible misfortunes befall him. He falls into a hot bath, is bitten by a huge dog, and falls from a tree. Because of his self-destructive impulses he beats himself up and is beaten by his father, who accuses his son of abandoning him. Mori does not will anything and lives in the unconscious. Since he does not know the function of language, he is equated with desocialization, but, by his very presence and innocence, he regenerates those around him.

This notion of ambivalence, the simultaneous presence of the negative and the positive, is also the focal point of Bakhtin's discussions of grotesque realism. He notes that "the grotesque image reflects a phenomenon in transformation, an as yet unfinished metamorphosis, of death and birth, growth and becoming. The relation to time is one determining trait of the grotesque image. The other indispensable trait is ambivalence. For in this image we find both poles of transformation, the old and the new, the dying and the procreating, the beginning and the end of the metamorphosis."[33]

Another element of ambivalence, the notion of a double, permeates many of the characters in the novel. For example, there is the case of the driver and his assistant, who exchange *manzai*-like (comic dialogue) verbal repartee during the nuclear hijacking; also the pair of policemen, one "conciliatory," the other, "a threatening type," who keep the father's house under twenty-four-hour surveillance. This antithetical pairing also extends to the two members of the Yamame Army whom the father nicknames Nōrifū (*the Able Official*) and Inutsura (*Dog Face*). Similarly, the existence of the Revolutionary Party is not quite complete without the presence of the Counter-Revolutionary Party. Finally, Ōno Sakurao, the woman counterpart of Gijin, represents along with the Yamame Army an ideal collectivity of civilian power.

Throughout *The Pinch-runner*, the transformed pair, Mori and the father, embodies this trait of ambivalence. The odd pair is portrayed as a double: "One brother normal, the other a dwarf!" the father once tells the ghost writer. Their transformation reinforces the ambivalent nature of the grotesque imagery because they each take the other's place. In the gathering of fifty buffoons, the pair disguised as a kangaroo baby and a wizard becomes the very embodiment of ambivalence: both poles of transformation, the old and the new, the dying and the procreating, the beginning and the end of the metamorphosis. At the same time, what the pair of buffoons, the father and the idiot son, possesses is "the clown-trickster intellect," which "informs us of the futility of clinging to one single reality. If the coercion of adhering to a single reality is the fate to which 'conformity' (*shubi ikkansei*) leads, to negate it is to live simultaneously divergent realities, to shuttle freely between them; the clown-trickster intellect, by its manifestation of these hidden realities, is the psychic technique of pioneering the more dynamic cosmic dimension."[34] This is how Ōe's Gargantua and Pantagruel continue a spiral journey into the world of the fantastic and grotesque realism, exploring potentials of a new cosmos and providing us at the same time with an entirely new outlook on the world.

8

In Search of Liminal Space and Time: *The Game of Contemporaneity*

In a prepublication interview with *Asahi Shimbun*, Ōe talked passionately about the concept of cultural negation central to the literary universe of *The Game of Contemporaneity* (Dōjidai gēmu, 1980, hereafter *Contemporaneity*).[1] By cultural negation, I mean the condition of being marginal and peripheral, which enables one to look at the "official" culture from the margins. It is the power "to confuse and to escape the structures of society and the order of cultural things."[2] Ōe implied that the 493-page narrative deals with "impossible possibilities, with endless caricatures, with reversals, negations, violations, and transformations"[3] that characterize the paradox of the world of the trickster:

> I was in India [when Mishima Yukio committed suicide]. I thought then that his suicide would bring about a revision of our history into one that centers around the Emperor. I wrote to an editor, a good friend of mine, that I would rather want to think about a god who did not obey the Emperor, and look at ancient times, medieval and modern times from the viewpoint of those who were chased outside, *expelled to the margins*. My novel started from that proposition. According to Yanagita Kunio [1875–1962], when the gods of the Imperial Family entered the scene, despite persistent resistance, the local gods were chased away. The gods of the disobedient nation [*matsurowanu kunitsukami*] went deep inside the forest and became demons. I attempted to write not a history that revolves around the Emperor, but a history that belongs to those who became demons.[4]

The mythological history of this disobedient nation begins when a group of dissident warriors (*bushi*), expelled from a fief (which Ōe disclosed as Tosa in his interview) on Shikoku, make an upstream, primordial journey on a river at night. Instead of the promised land of milk and honey, they encounter a "huge rock, or a black solid mass of soil" that blocks their way. An atrocious stench assaults their nostrils as the rebel band leader, called *The One Who Destroys* (*Kowasu hito*), blasts the rock to smithereens with gun powder. For the next fifty days, torrential rains come down continuously, washing everything away including the poisonous air. On the fiftieth day, the rain stops and the *bushi* and *The One Who Destroys* discover before them a fertile, uninhabited basin and a clear river, whereupon they set to work to construct a new nation called the village=nation=minicosmos (and often referred to as the valley and the "country").

The people during the Construction Period grow into giants and live more than one hundred years, *The One Who Destroys* over 500 years. The newly built ancient community enjoys total independence and freedom until the end of the Tokugawa Shōgunate (1860s), when a *bushi* on his way to Kyoto accidentally spots the hidden basin. At the same time, some peasants who have organized an uprising in the downstream region flee farther up the river and discover the hidden hamlet. To overcome the dual crisis, the villagers charge the young Kamei Meisuke, who leads the diplomatic corps, first to negotiate with the Shōgunate officials, and second to mediate between the peasant rebels and the authorities. The villagers also invent a dual registration system. Whenever a baby is born, they wait for the birth of another and register only one of the babies in the official registry. The result is that only half of the village population belongs to the Great Empire of Japan. Just before the China Incident (1937) the village fights the Fifty-Day War against the Imperial Army and surrenders unconditionally in the end. The village, now in decline, awaits yet another resurrection of *The One Who Destroys*, who has met many deaths during his long life.

The key to understanding Ōe's mythological world is found in Victor Turner's notion of "liminality" and "structure/anti-structure." Based on Arnold van Gennep's definition of a three-phase "ritual process," Turner's theory amplifies the symbolic meaning of the rite of passage—separation, margin (*limen*, threshold in Latin), and reaggregation. In times of transition—"every change of state or social position, or certain points in age"—an initiand detaches himself from his social group.[5] During the "separation" he goes through the intervening "liminal" period in which he becomes ambiguous, neither here nor there, "betwixt and between all fixed points of classification" set up by law, custom, convention, and ceremonial.[6] In reaggregation, the rite of passage is consummated and the ritual subject reenters the social structure at a high level.[7]

What is of particular interest to us in our examination of the characters and the world of the village=nation=minicosmos is the second phase of the ritual process, "liminality." The "betwixt and between" state of liminality generates what Turner calls "communitas," a modality of interrelatedness, of an "unstructured or rudimentarily structured and relatively undifferentiated *comitatus*, community, or even communion of equal individuals who submit together to the general authority of the ritual elders."[8]

Communitas is directly opposed to the concept of social structure, the patterned arrangements of roles and statuses "*consciously* recognized and regularly operative in a given society."[9] This "closed" society nurtures itself on "a structured, differentiated, and often hierarchical system of political-legal economic positions with many types of evaluation, separating men in terms of 'more' or 'less'."[10] In other words, a differentiated segmented system of structured positions relies heavily on the "jural-political power of the strong" whereas the "power of the weak" is nourished by the undifferentiated whole of communitas.

Three common characteristics of liminality, Turner notes, are "persons or principles that (1) fall in the interstices of social structure, (2) are on its margins, or, (3) occupy its lowest rungs."[11] He amplifies these points and discusses several aspects of the relationship between liminality, "outsiderhood," and "structural inferiority." Liminality, referring to the "midpoint of transition in a status-sequence between two positions," produces structural invisibility in terms of human cultural classifications. "Outsiderhood," means the physical removal from the social structure, the "condition of being either permanently or by ascription set outside the structural arrangements of a given social system, or being . . . set apart, or . . . setting oneself apart from the behavior of status-occupying, role-playing members of that system."[12] "Structural inferiority" refers to occupying the lowest rung of a society, the despised and rejected in general, stripped of status and rank, whose symbolic function is to represent humanity as a whole.

The traits and attributes of liminality characterize Ōe's disobedient nation, explaining the antinomian behavior and existence of the people in the village=nation=minicosmos. Originally, the founding fathers were outcasts, expelled to the sea by the authorities in the hope that they would be shipwrecked. After they discovered a hidden basin and created a new nation, they consistently chose to maintain the condition of "outsiderhood," of being cast on the margins of society. Protected by the vast virgin forest, the village literally falls into the interstice of social structure, and the inhabitants remain invisible to the outer world, their objective being to attain the status of "missing persons." Unlike ritual liminars, they are marginals who have no recourse to reenter the society they were unwillingly detached from, and no means to resolve the state of ambiguity, of the "neither here nor there" situation.

The central issue raised by the existence of the antistructural nation is the absurd, unthinkable idea of political independence demanded by a small, insignificant village on Shikoku. Ōe both pokes fun at and laments the fact that, for the majority of Japanese, the notion of political freedom at the cost of countless lives lost in bloodshed, or a secession (as the original state constitution declared in the law of the State of Texas) from the benevolent Imperial nation, is as absurd as consuming cooked rice with milk and sugar. The case of the small island of Okinawa illustrates this very "impossible possibility." In the aftermath of World War II, the Okinawans had a perfect opportunity to secede from the mainland. However, despite their enormous cultural differences and the Japanese discriminations against them, they had to accept unwillingly the reunification with a motherland whose attitude toward her stepchild has never been of a reassuring nature.

In chapter 8 in *The Method of a Novel*, "To the Margins, From the Margins' (*Shūen e, shūen kara*), Ōe analyzes the peripheral position of Okinawa vis-à-vis the centrality of the Emperor-centered mainland, Japan. Returned to Japan after a quarter-century of American occupation, Okinawa also regained its administrative rights and came under Japanese sovereignty in 1972. Ōe talks about an unprecedented incident that involved the Crown Prince and Princess, who visited Okinawa on July 17, 1975, to attend the opening ceremony of the Ocean Exposition 75. When the royal couple paid homage to the famous "Tower of Lilies" (*Himeyuri no tō*), a fifteen-meter-deep underground air-raid shelter where many young Okinawan women, prevented by the Imperial Army from surrendering, killed themselves during the American invasion, two young radicals hiding in the dark pit threw a Molotov cocktail.[13] Ōe points out that tossing the "hand-made" grenade was a symbolic act because the assailants made sure beforehand it would endanger no one's life. In the meantime the crowd began to whistle. Ōe calls our attention to its significance: "Whistling in Okinawa is an expression of festivity communicating applause and encouragement.''[14] The function of the Crown Prince's visit was to formally announce the absorption of the Okinawans into the cultural domain of the Emperor-centered mainland. At the same time the "Molotov'' incident attests to the marginality of the Okinawan position—one which counters the "central'' position occupied by the Emperor—and also to the Okinawans' desire to confirm their state of being outside the cultural domain of the mainland, and therefore to place the center in a critical perspective.[15]

"The shift from the absolutist Emperor System in the old Constitution to the symbolic Emperor System,'' Ōe continues, "was far from accomplishing'' the diffusion of the power of the cultural sphere headed by the Emperor. "Neither has it functioned as an impetus to create another cultural domain'' that will express a marginal consciousness freed from the center of the Emperor System. "All of the mainlanders are within the confines of the cultural sphere governed by the Emperor System. Under these circumstances, a cultural hero like the trickster in the pit who played a provoking prank on the Crown Prince . . . has never appeared on the mainland.''[16]

Behind the assessment of the Okinawan issue is Ōe's deep concern for the peculiar absence of a potential for communitas. What underlies the composition of *Contemporaneity* is his quest for and powerful dream of a different kind of nation, whose inhabitants are allowed to see the earth, the sun, the galaxy, and the cosmos from the margins to the margins. One such inhabitant is Private Tsuyukazu. The narrator's oldest brother, after developing a mental disorder during basic training in the Imperial Army, spends twenty-five years in a mental institution, and later stages a "revolt'' to settle the issue of Japan's unconditional surrender. This episode of Private Tsuyukazu's "solitary revolt'' illustrates Ōe's keen insight and liberated intellect, which enable him to take a sober look at sociopolitical issues still fresh in his and our memories, to "defamiliarize'' them, and still manage to provoke festive laughter.

Temporarily allowed to disembark from the Narrenschiff, "The Ship of Fools,'' Private Tsuyukazu one day finds himself at a mountain lodging. In his mind's eye the room is an army barracks where he received daily beatings. He salutes each of the five beds in the room, believing his five roommates are his comrades-in-arms. When one of them strikes him in the face, the blow revives in him more than ever the reality of barracks life:

> Although it was already mid-October, he did not wear the overcoat which he tied to the knapsack together with a tent, a hand flag, and a spoon. He carefully put the puttees around his legs and equipped himself with a belt sword, a canteen, a duffle bag, and a gas mask. As he was about to leave the room with a fatigue hat on his head, army shoes in his right hand and a rifle in the left, the roommates wide awake by this time all cheered his departure singing a war song: "We left the country bravely vowing we would win / We cannot die without glory in battle / Whenever we hear the marching bugle. . . . (398)

At 12:00 noon he stands facing the forest of the Imperial Palace (*Kōkyo no mori*). (The Emperor's broadcast on the termination of the war was aired exactly at 12:00 noon.) Ōe's Don Quixote encounters many obstacles before he can carry out his plans: he runs into three American hippies whom he holds hostage for three hours. At night when he puts up a tent in the plaza of the Imperial Palace, two intruders disturb his sleep—a couple making love in the open air. Private Tsuyukazu succeeds in chasing them away, but he must deal with another wave of invasion: this time a group of black-garbed voyeurs. Totally displeased with the abrupt *coitus interruptus*, they kick and pommel him. "When they turned on their flashlights, there loomed up before them, a skinny middle-aged man in a military uniform" (402).

The following morning, Private Tsuyukazu resumes his march, on all fours, which continues from morning till noon until the security police spot him. However, he succeeds in penetrating the "enemy" blockade and runs inside the Imperial Palace gate carrying a rifle with a white flag attached to it. His mission: to request an audience with the Emperor and demand the right of the village=nation=minicosmos to secede from Japan!

In a medley of parody, satire, travesty, and grotesque realism, *Contemporaneity* continues its lampoon of the Imperial Army in another episode, "Brilliant Deeds of Arms: the Fifty-Day War," a war which of course has never been recorded in official history. This is an embarrassing war for the Imperial Army, because the first company in hot pursuit of the insubordinate Japanese drowns in the "black" flood artificially caused by the invisible enemy who blast away the river dam with dynamite. Marching along the raging river in the "black" downpour, how could the officers retreat and report to their superiors,

"——The Imperial Army has proven to be no match for the cumulative strength of the torrential rains stored in the forest, sir!" (263)? The flood not only wipes out the entire company, but causes extensive damage to the region downstream. The national authorities issue a statement directed to those suffering in the flood that the damage is slight, that there is hardly a flood; they pass down a strict order to maintain silence about the disaster.[17]

One officer is assigned the task of promoting and sending the dead officers and soldiers to distant battlefields in China and Southeast Asia so that their deaths can be reported publicly and their families notified formally. "Captain No-Name's" primary objective is to plan the whole war in such a way that he can erase any trace of the Imperial Army in the valley and therefore show that he had never existed in the army as an individual soldier: "——This is going to be a long war, the Captain said to himself resolutely. . . . Once the war is over, he would have to make his officers and men, and the residents of the basin who fought as their enemy, believe that the war was just a groundless rumor spread by agitators from Mainland China and the Pacific Region. . . " (276).[18]

Totally in a daze as to the purpose of the rebels' resistance, "Captain No-Name" must fight a passive war against the invisible enemy: the first company drowned, one NCO killed, four soldiers attacked and disarmed, five soldiers having lost their legs in traps. The Fifty-Day War is an embarrassing mishap to the Great Empire of Japan for another reason: while the public is giving full support for expansionism, this insignificant village in the valley is putting up a fight against the almighty Imperial Army, insisting that the village does not belong to the Great Empire of Japan. Antinationalistic sentiment must be eradicated at any cost without the knowledge of the public. "The national authority which declared war on the village=nation=minicosmos obliterated all the data concerning the Fifty-Day War, did everything to strike out evidence, and cracked down on freedom of speech" (253).

The elders of the village=nation=minicosmos have a different reason behind their wish to "cooperate willingly with the Great Empire of Japan in their efforts to obliterate from history all the facts concerning the Fifty-Day War" (253). By consenting to the obliteration of their history, they are actually asserting that they are outside the cultural domain of the Great Empire of Japan, and that they have nothing to do with the authorities. As marginals, they are "structurally if not physically invisible in terms of [their] culture's definitions and classifications.''[19] The Fifty-Day War is a ''fantasy'' war (according to the official verson of history) that had never happened, but had to happen for the rebels to ''prove to the Imperial Army the existence of the village=nation=minicosmos, by hurling at the Great Empire of Japan the device of dual registration that still had been maintained until that time'' (280). In other words, the rebels flaunt their marginality by revealing the means of hiding half of their population, the dual registry.

How does this rebel army fight back? When the second company led by ''Captain No-Name'' occupies the valley, still drenched in the ''black'' water, the people of the village=nation=minicosmos hide inside the ''big ocean of the forest'' with all their cattle and dogs. One of the most democratic armies in the history of military organizations, the guerrillas' mobile war cabinet is made up of the elders, the quartermaster corps of young women, the guerrilla army units of young men, the munitions factory of children and women, with older couples bringing up the rear in mobile tents. Under the leadership of *The One Who Destroys*, who gives them instructions in dreams, the guerrillas harass the Imperial Army with flexible tactics. In the daylight they counter man-hunting tactics with flying columns. At night, they set up European hunting traps modified to catch human beings. Their weapons factory in the depths of the forest manufactures super-sophisticated arms made out of recycled German toys. They show ''highly ethical principles in their fighting tactics which include their decision not to poison the drinking water to which they had allowed the Imperial Army to gain access. The guerrillas at times played pranks, not contrary to their *esprit de corps*, that would elicit laughter'' (290).

''Captain No-Name's'' frustration, despair, and shame mount day by day, and he must confront *The One Who Destroys* in his dreams and reveries:

> The minute ''Captain No-Name'' tried to sleep, there appeared in his dreams *The One Who Destroys*, who shifted his gaze down to the liver-shaped lump of shame that was attached to the chest of ''Captain No-Name's'' uniform as a reversed medal. . . . After the repeated dream assaults, ''Captain No-Name'' began to show signs of examining the liver of shame on his uniform even while awake. To pacify his subordinates who were suspicious of his behavior, he made a bag out of the purple silk that wrapped his sword, stuffed it into the shape of a liver, and attached it to his uniform. However, still none of his men had any idea that the purple silk was not a medal made for his pleasure, but was rather a lump of shame that proliferated like cancer until it surfaced on the skin. (334)

Here, the main theme of *The Scarlet Letter*, religious hypocrisy accompanied by psychological trauma, seems to be embedded in this story of a hand-made "purple heart."

In their ridiculous belief, the rebels imagine that their land is equal to the entire territory of the Great Empire of Japan: " 'Captain No-Name's' next move is to comb every inch of the forest." His goal is, after all, the "geographical conquest of the entire forest which maintains the myth and history of the village = nation = minicosmos from the margins and has taken everyone under its wing" (314). He draws a twenty-degree line radially on the one-fifty-thousandth-scale map; if he did this eighteen times, he would have covered the entire forest. Already informed by *The One Who Destroys* of the new tactics of the enemy, the whole guerrilla force moves further into the interior of the forest, leaving the weapons factory completely vacated by the time the Imperial Army officers inspect the building.

His weakness being "defensive perfectionism," "Captain No-Name" immediately undertakes the destruction of the munitions plant. He orders his men to chop gigantic trees down and clear the earth "100 meters by 2.5 meters in width straight to the site of the factory from the location of the headquarters" (330). Personally in charge of the field artillery, he opens fire on the factory, blowing it to smithereens:

> The officers and men of the Great Empire of Japan cheered at their great victory. What then followed under the noses of these officers and men shouting banzai twice, three times, their fighting spirit inflamed by the futile act of destruction? . . . They saw the rebels of the forest, over one hundred in number, revealing themselves all at once. A chorus of mocking laughter replaced the shouts of joy. . . . However, what they were witnessing in derision was the fire-fighting task force, each emerging from the groves with a canvas bucket in his hand, putting out the fire that was blazing in the destroyed shack and the trees and vegetation that surrounded it. (331)

Both the Fifty-Day War and Private Tsuyukazu's "revolt," portrayed in the festive laughter of the oral tradition, illustrate one of several literary genres *Contemporaneity* tries to explore: a satire on the official version of history sanctioned by the national authority. Side by side with the satiric is the parodic, which Ōe employs to create the mythical world of *The One Who Destroys*. *Contemporaneity* parodies epics and creation myths, particularly Japanese mythology, in which the Imperial Family is said to have descended from the Sun Goddess,

Amaterasu Ōmikami. Furthermore, the narrative displays the brilliant technique of oral tradition, by incorporating words from the dialect of Ōe's birth place and explaining their etymology.[20] He derives almost all of the materials on myth and folklore from what he as a child heard and dreamed about in his native village: "In *The Game of Contemporaneity* I let it all hang out, things I had reveries on or thought about."[21]

Contemporaneity starts off from what the Japanese creation myth leaves undeveloped. In other words, the myth of the village=nation= minicosmos is a "sacred" narrative that tells of the marginals represented by Hiruko, the legless firstborn of the World Parents, Izanagi and Izanami, who banished the deformed baby in a reed boat into the marginal world.[22] Ōe deals with the concepts of marginality and deformity with respect to Mexico, constantly comparing what the narrator experiences in Mexico with the myth and history of the village=nation=minicosmos: "Since I had the toothache and the revelation in Malinako, the details of my life in Mexico have begun to resonate, from the deep waters of the subconscious to the shallows in the sun of consciousness, with each and every experience I had in our land" (81). The art of a Mexican painter, Posada, the narrator discovers, is synonymous with marginality and "structural inferiority" and portrays in woodblock prints calamities such as flood, fire, epidemic, and the birth of a deformed baby. In the eye of the narrator, the deformed baby Hiruko's tiny reed boat transforms itself into the Narrenschiff, "The Ship of Fools," which "haunted the imagination of the entire early Renaissance, . . . pilgrimage boats, highly symbolic cargoes of madmen in search of their reason."[23] Cast forever outside the limits of human society, the ships must roam from one port to another.

Ōe emphasizes the mythic aspect of the boat metaphor in the rapid succession of symbolic inversions the boat undergoes during the nocturnal journey of the founding fathers and the tribal chief, *The One Who Destroys*. The narrator posits the central question: why did the founding fathers hamper themselves by using only the original materials of the ship?

> Despite the fact that they were expelled from the port, the outcast crew of the Narrenschiff, *outsmarting* (*ura o kaite*) the fief authorities who hoped they would vanish into the depths of the sea, cruised countless times near the coast, running the risk of grounding their boat, and, no sooner had they found the hidden river mouth than they went steadily upstream. Once the ship began to scrape the river bottom, they dismantled the rigging, remodeled the hull, and continued the upstream journey. When running

rapids which the ship could not navigate, they dismantled the hull and reassembled it as a raft. . . . As they had *reversed* the function of a raft, which is to passively float along down the river, the founding fathers and *The One Who Destroys turned* things *in their favor* [*gyakuten sasete*] and continued to go upstream. . . . When the authorities expelled them in the hope that they would be shipwrecked, they *turned* the no-way-out dilemma *around* [*hikkuri kaeshite*] into the potential for life. This was the purpose of the Narrenschiff. They also made a raft out of the ship lumber; when it entered the mountain stream that would not let in the wide raft, they reconverted it into a narrow sleigh-like raft. That they did not abandon the materials of the original Narrenschiff was a symbolic act with a clear meaning. (25)[24]

The careful selection of those words that express the idea of impossible possibilities, reversals, violations, and transformations defines the very nature of the symbolic world of *Contemporaneity* in its liminal space and time. Beyond the control of the clock, liminal time is "a time of enchantment when anything *might*, even should, happen."[25] Travelling on a river which is "a road *turned upside down* [*sakasama no*]," and travelling only at night because the "river at night proved to be the *wrong side* [*urakaeshi*] of the road in the daylight," the founding fathers undergo the symbolic process of time reversal: "Their journey upstream through the waterway, intensifying their solitude from the outer world.[26] It was also a journey through the passage of time for the founding fathers led by *The One Who Destroys*. From modern to medieval, and then to ancient times, *The One Who Destroys* and the founding fathers, journeying in silence in the darkness of night, retraced the past as if unwinding at terrifying speed the passage of time" (194).

As they go farther upstream, they begin to smell a horrible stench and encounter the "huge rock, or the black solid mass of soil," which, the narrator tells us, was probably "the gods' excrement, the concretization of interdiction" (99). In other words, the blasting of the rock by the rebel leader marks the transgressive activity of a trickster, "The Foolish One," who violates a taboo "in order to satisfy the needs and aspirations of his group."[27] As a breaker of taboos, *The One Who Destroys* shares many of the traits attributed to the trickster. He is given full license to ignore prohibitions and break them, tends to be multiform and ambiguous, often appears in scatological and coprophagous episodes which may be creative, destructive, or simply amusing, and wanders around dwelling at crossroads. Often "indeterminant," he is portrayed as both young and old; he is destructive, creative, farcical, aggressive, defiant of authority, but always unpredictable.[28]

First of all, Ōe portrays the farcical *The One Who Destroys* as a character endowed with both destructive and creative power. In the blasting of the "huge rock, or the black solid mass of soil," he suffers from third-degree burns. Charred completely black, he wears eye-patches and crawls quietly into a pit to regenerate himself. The narrator tells us why this disaster has befallen him: "What has been transmitted to us as a myth is that because the fuse was not quite long enough, *The One Who Destroys* could not get away in time, and was charred as black as the wall he blasted" (97). In addition to expertise in demolition (use of gun powder) and civil engineering, he has medical knowledge: he orders an herbal concoction to be made as an ointment for his burns and lies down, still black, for fifty days until he has completely recovered. The dominant color symbolism, black, which has come to be associated with him, indicates destructiveness and death, yet he is also a healer and many-lived. But he is also capable of reversing his behavior. He later turns into a tyrant, mistreats his own people, and imprisons the founding fathers.[29] In the end he totally forgets human speech. The resentment among the people accumulates until they conspire to assassinate him. His body is cut up into 300 parts "like seed potatoes," and everyone, from the old to the infant, partakes of a piece of his minced flesh. What we see in the life story of *The One Who Destroys* is creative destruction, or the "sacredness of transgression,"[30] associated with trickster tales.

Like a trickster, *The One Who Destroys* is unpredictable and home-less. The people of the village=nation=minicosmos never know when and where they should expect him. He often appears in dreams to instruct his people prior to the occurrences of major sociopolitical events. For example, in the beginning of May in the year when the Fifty-Day War breaks out between the village=nation=minicosmos and the Great Empire of Japan, the elders see at dawn the identical dream in which they learn that *The One Who Destroys*, who has been away for a long time, is back in the wax storehouse that stands in the center of the village:

> . . . *The One Who Destroys*, who grew into a giant, his back big as a small mountain, turned away from them, moved his huge head slowly around and gave instructions as follows. ——Within a month and a half the governor will request the mobilization of security forces by flaunting

the Article, "IN CASE OF AN EMERGENCY THAT MAY REQUIRE ARMED FORCE, SUBMIT A REQUEST FOR THE DISPATCH OF TROOPS TO THE DIVISION COMMANDER OR NOTIFY THE BRIGADIER GENERAL!" You must stop up the "neck" of the valley with rocks and soil, and fill the valley with water to open a counter-offensive. Unless you bury the "neck" of the valley with a bulldozer, and finish the task in twenty days, you'll get bogged down in the rainy season" (255).

The only physical evidence of *The One Who Destroys*'s presence is shown in the first and last "telephone conversation" that takes place between the two commanding officers of the Fifty-Day War, "Captain No-Name" of the Imperial Army and *The One Who Destroys*:

> "Captain No-Name" placed a call to Regimental Headquarters. However the first voice reverberating through the receiver that he pressed hard against his ear sounded decidedly admonitory. ——You've started an unprofitable war, yessir! Don't bother with us and just get out of the valley tomorrow morning! the voice said. The voice of an old man of discretion and quick action, "Captain No-Name" could only guess belonged to an uneducated mad oldster, but neither could the Captain dismiss in the voice the resourcefulness of a superb commanding officer. The telephone went dead, and when "Captain No-Name" blasted off to the NCO of the engineering corps, ——What the hell's going on? the electricity went out. A big explosion shook the ground, informing the entire Imperial Army occupying the valley that the cable had been bombed and cut off. (292)

Everything goes wrong for the enemy commander-in-chief, whose "clever" tactics are no match for the "hocus-pocus" counter-offensive designed and organized by the trickster, *The One Who Destroys*. The frustrated "Captain No-Name" resolves to defoliate the virgin forest: " ——I will burn down the whole forest, not a blade of grass or a tree shall remain!" (342). At this point the environmentalist-rebel army surrenders unconditionally preserving the vast forest that surrounds the hidden basin referred to as the valley and the "country."

Ōe's mythical trickster, *The One Who Destroys*, who leads the rebel army against the Great Empire of Japan, also serves as the ruler of the underworld, the god of darkness. The cosmology of the village=nation=minicosmos reveals that the hidden basin has a distinctive shape, that of a jar. Burial in a clay jar was one of the forms of interment performed by ancient Japanese; a famous "keyhole" burial mound built for Emperors in ancient times suggests a variation of the jar shape. The village = nation = minicosmos is a gigantic coffin, a country of the dead, a forbidden place into which nobody has set foot for several hundred years. The narrator speculates on the possibility of the outside world's knowledge of the new world: "Suppose the outsiders gave a wide berth to the people in our land who disappeared into the underworld alive, because they knew our people were leading a disreputable life in an infamous place, the dead buried in a huge jar coffin; then the isolated peace among the children of the dead who prospered in the underworld could be explained very easily" (221). This cosmic layout of the village = nation = minicosmos establishes the position of the disobedient god as the ruler of darkness which counters the sun goddess, Amaterasu, of the Imperial ancestors.

The jar-keyhole shape also represents the mythical fusion of male and female, suggesting the concept of androgyny or hermaphroditism[31] as shown in the Japanese folk worship of Dōsojin.[32] Ōe explores the concept of two-in-one in *Contemporaneity* through the "ambivalence of the mythical couple of brother and sister"[33] and twinship.

The now-declined village = nation = minicosmos, in anticipation of the resurrection of *The One Who Destroys*, has been blessed with the birth of twins, one to serve as chronicler, the other as the vestal virgin, the keeper of the village = nation = minicosmos' myth and history. As Turner points out in his discussion of Ndembu tribal ritual, twinship presents the "paradoxes that what is physically double is structurally single and what is mystically one is empirically two."[34] Twinship shows at its best the "process whereby *two become one* . . . [and] the converse of this, the process whereby one becomes two, [is] the process of bifurcation."[35] The twin-brother-narrator of *Contemporaneity* who regards the notion of 2 = 1 as holy, lets this concept dictate his entire life. But, in fact, the myth and history of the village = nation = minicosmos would not have been written at all had it not been for his allegiance to or his feeling for his twin sister. "I finally found somebody else who's lived my life like those days of *The One Who Destroys*, my little twin sister." (8)

A pair of opposites underlies the three basic features of *Contemporaneity*: the relationship of the twins, the cosmology of the village = nation = minicosmos, and the framework of the narrative discourse. And as we have seen, the binary oppositions of male/female, life/death, light/darkness, etc., function multivocally, a single image or symbol designating simultaneously many different meanings.

Parodying the almost identical names of the Japanese mythological couple, Izanagi and Izanami (brother and sister), who created the Japanese islands, Ōe adopts twinship as a means of debunking the authorities of Imperial Japan. The twin brother, the scribe of the myth and history of the village=nation=minicosmos, writes to his twin sister that the all-out war fought against the Great Empire of Japan has been totally expunged from the history of the outside world: " . . . whatever evidence that has survived as historical documents can be found in the way they entered us twins in the family registry. The eccentricity of the registry lies in the fact that our names look almost identical on paper. Tsuyuki, Tsuyumi. It was no coincidence. . . . We were the first babies to be born after the Fifty-Day War, and by capitalizing on the twin birth, the elders of the village=nation=minicosmos retaliated against the victor, the Great Empire of Japan'' (248).

Two-in-one, or one-becomes-two, is also basic to the structure of the narrative discourse, the epistolary format adopted by Ōe. The opening paragraph of the ''epistolary novel'' tells us two things central to the narrative: the narrator has been trying to start a project, and he is dwelling on a method most suitable to write his project. ''My little sister, ever since I could remember, I've always thought about the project I'd one day start writing. Once I started on it, by the method I have at last hit upon, I firmly believed that I'd continue to write it without losing my way, but hesitated until now to start writing'' (7).

The project involves recording in print the myth and history of the narrator's land, and for this he adopts an epistolary form, writing directly to his twin sister, and indirectly to *The One Who Destroys*. The narrator's six letters are constantly ''punctuated'' by ''my little sister'' (*imōto yo*), which indicates in Japanese that he is directly ''speaking'' to his sister. The self-reflexivity of writing is more apparent in letter writing in that it requires *two* persons, the sender and receiver of the code, for a personal letter to fulfill its function. Public documents, travelogues, or narratives, on the other hand, assume a readership of more than one person. It is absolutely necessary for the twin-brother-narrator to be interconnected and fused with his twin sister in every way possible. His decision to accept the role of chronicler comes concomitantly with his twin sister's taking on the duties of a vestal virgin of *The One Who Destroys*.

My little sister, even through the letter I received in Mexico, I knew you've accepted the role of a vestal virgin. I've heard that you've found *The One Who Destroys* in hibernation, small as a dried-up mushroom in the "pit," resurrected him and restored him to a size as big as a dog. When I think about you, that you'll be reading the myth and history in this epistolary fashion holding *The One Who Destroys* on your lap, that thought becomes an endless source of inspiration. The entirety of the village=nation=minicosmos completed by the gigantic *The One Who Destroys* will be received by you, the vestal virgin, holding on your lap *The One Who Destroys*, big as a dog. . . . I feel it is a marvelous reaggregation of the beginning and the end so that they merge into a large orbit. (112)

The twin brother sends a letter, and the twin sister receives it. He writes a letter and she reads it. It takes *two* to create *one*.

The narrator owns a color slide of the twin sister's "flaming pubic hair," the source of energy and encouragement for him to complete the project. Apart from this erotic image, the other side of her "crotch," the "light cream-colored buttocks," becomes the narrator's irresistible fascination: the image of bifurcation, one-becomes-two in the duality of twinship. To be the other half of her (bifurcation), and to become one with her (unification), are his constant dream and obsession. For example, when he mentions an owner of a small iron factory and his unfinished "hibernation machine," the memory immediately sparks an image of a "steel sheath": "I wanted him to take you and me with him in the steel sheath, both of us in one sheath, going back into the womb where we once coexisted" (121).

It is not so much his fear of incest as the fact that he is the "other half" of her that prevents him from attaining consummation in a sexual union with her. He is therefore driven to seek it with other women. In one of his affairs, a most ideal "position" brings him and his partner together in the mystical unity of opposites: "The woman and I had finally settled ourselves into the position we wanted. As she lay on her back her legs spread loosely apart, I placed by buttocks at an angle underneath hers and her right thigh. As my belly touched her buttocks which were twisted slightly to the left, I inserted my penis. In a slow thrust my right hand stroked time after time the spot where the vagina held the penis in between and over the mound of Venus, the way a woman caresses her own vagina" (251). What the narrator aims at is the superimposition of two bodies, a male and a female, complementary to each other yet in fusion. "Inside the vagina sizzling like hot water I felt that I had become one with her. Making love to and masturbating myself, trying to come to the orgasm of the woman. In happy peacefulness she and I were transformed into one and became you'' (252).

In what the narrator calls "the sections deleted from the first epistle prior to the mailing," he tells us how he once tried to seduce his twin sister: "When you realized what I wanted, you changed the tactics of resistance. Extending one arm lithely from behind, you held my penis gently in your hand and made me ejaculate" (88). She says to him that the whole thing is like the "game" of *The One Who Destroys*. The game consists of selecting a boy for *The One Who Destroys*, who gets into one of the pits in the forest. The rest of the children are encouraged to break taboos and do things normally prohibited or impossible. Some children walk around exhibiting transvestism, some defecate wherever they please. In liminal space and time, symbolizations of transgressive acts such as an incestuous union of brother and sister, the eating of human flesh (the minced flesh of *The One Who Destroys*), transvestism, scatology, are intimately tied into the "primary or primordial generative powers of the cosmos."[36]

As Ōe constructs the world of the mythic and satiric by unfolding the myth and history of the village=nation=minicosmos, he presents us with three versions of the myth and history which reveal a reconstructive process the reader must undergo to grasp the totality of *Contemporaneity*. The narrator's father, called "father=priest," is responsible for the first version, which he has based on life-long research. As the official transmitter of oral tradition, the father=priest dwells on the highest *topos* in the valley and drills his son in this myth and history. He opens his tutorial sessions with a formulaic line: "*Familiar stories. We don't know whether they existed or didn't exist. Since they're tales of days gone by, we've got to pretend they existed when they may not have existed. Get it?*" followed by an automatic response, "*Yup!*" (94).

The second version of the myth and history comes from what a peasant community as a whole hands down from generation to generation. The third one represents, as we have seen, what the reader finds in the text of the novel, the six letters the narrator writes to his twin sister from Mexico, the written records of the mythology of the village=nation=minicosmos made richer by the chronicler's imagination, research, and inspiration. The result is the narrator's own version, what he believes it must have been and must be, which is later fully supported by the father=priest.

All three versions evoke the festive laughter of oral tradition, the "popular laughter" in which M. M. Bakhtin seeks the "authentic folkloric roots of the novel."[37] Comparing the fundamental differences between the epic and the novel, "the official" and "the unofficial," Bakhtin analyzes the "common people's creative culture of laughter" (p. 20), which destroys the form of epic, whose past is absolute and complete, whose world has no place "for any openendedness, indecision, indeterminacy. There are no loopholes in it through which we glimpse the future" (p. 16). Revealed and preserved only in the form of national tradition, the world of epic is an "utterly finished thing, not only as an authentic event of the distant past but also on its own terms and by its own standards; it is impossible to change, to re-think, to re-evaluate anything in it" (p. 17). On the contrary, rethinking and reevaluating the present is at the core of the world of the novel: "To portray an event on the same time-and-value plane as oneself and one's contemporaries (and an event that is therefore based on personal experience and thought) is to undertake a radical revolution, and to step out of the world of epic into the world of the novel." (p. 14)

The legend of Oshikome in *Contemporaneity*, in which Ōe combines the mythic and the satiric in popular laughter, illustrates this radical revolution. By means of this legend, Ōe superimposes the past on the present, on the same time-and-value plane as our contemporaries. Oshikome, the oldest and the last wife of *The One Who Destroys*, is the wire-puller of a counterrevolution that shakes the sociopolitical foundation of the village=nation=minicosmos one hundred years after its construction. The ancient society, originally based on communal ownership and polyandry, gradually evolves into an ordinary settlement made up of privately owned property. A loud, mysterious sound like the earth tremor that once assaulted the founding fathers for one hundred days "revisits" the basin. The second powerful sound lasts for fifty days. In the beginning it is a small boom, not unpleasant, and depending on the place, the quality and the volume of the sound differ. The incident, called the "Restoration Movement," stimulates a total re-structuring of social relationships, including the abolition of private property. First, the children become hypersensitive to the sound, and they unite with young men (fourteen to eighteen years old) to intervene energetically with the adults in the changing of shelter (*sumikae*), breaking up and regrouping family members.

At first people regard their new grouping as a temporary arrangement, believing that some supernatural being is behind it all. However, the young men's group begins to persecute those families who refuse to be separated. The angry youngsters burn down the offenders' houses and massacre those who try to escape the basin. *The One Who Destroys*'s widow, Oshikome, who engineers the "Restoration Movement," seizes power as the successor of her husband in a newly formed cabinet.

A master hand at political satire, Ōe seems to be replaying the historical events of the "Cultural Revolution" and the "Gang of Four" in a mythological setting. Atrocity in history translates as symbolic fertility in myths. The fire started by the young arsonists spreads to the surrounding groves, but not to the virgin forest: ". . . the fire revitalized the land overused by one hundred years of farming, and also burned out the energy that supported the 'Restoration Movement' " (160). This counterrevolutionary movement is also the period of a brawl, a sexual orgy held by Oshikome:

> Oshikome, who thought the fecundity of the land was diminished by the loud mysterious sound, felt the need to perform a ritual to revitalize the reproductive power of the fields. She stripped off her waistcloth, the only garb worn by women in the land, and lay down on the ground. Her body, swelled into gigantic proportions as big as a small mountain, and despite her one hundred years of age, maintained a softness and voluptuousness that aroused all the young men in her company into a sexual frenzy. Twenty young men clung to the amazon who spread out on the great nocturnal earth reclining on one arm, and, as desire exploded within her, had sexual intercourse with the stars that bedecked the heavens. (143)

In the end Oshikome's atrocious crimes are exposed, her power removed, and she is pushed into one of the "pits" in the forest (her name is a pun on "hag" and "a female demon" and a verb, "to squeeze someone/something into"). The "Restoration Movement," however, drastically revolutionized the social, economic, and political structure of the village=nation=minicosmos during Oshikome's reign of terror. In addition to eliminating rank and status, it also destroyed the ethical bond that unites a wife absolutely to her husband, advancing the cause of Women's Liberation!

Popular laughter bellowing at living reality, and popular speech rooted in folklore tradition, make it possible to "contemporize" the epic past of the founding fathers and *The One Who Destroys*, a world of "beginnings" and "golden times." Ōe attempts to deliver the past, present, and future into the "hands of free experimental fantasy" (p. 23), or in Turner's words, to analyze "culture into factors and their free combination in any and every possible pattern.''[38] *Contemporaneity* revels in this pattern making, with the philosophy of a card game, whose basic feature lies in the almost unlimited experimentation with recombining and regrouping of a deck of cards. At the end of *Contemporaneity*, the narrator-chronicler illustrates this freedom to recombine history (the recollection of past events) in terms of contemporaneity, rethinking and reevaluating the present. Upon learning the existence of a three-dimensional space, a world made up of a unit, space x time, the young myth-writer tells something of a science fiction story about a spaceship that can reach all the planets in the cosmos in one flash: ''Suppose we can see an infinite number of units, space x time, that exist on an infinite number of planets, then the eyeball that views these units is actually witnessing the entire history of mankind on the earth, all the events taking place simultaneously. Provided that's the case, the eyeball can also select a reality at will, like a game, among an infinite number of units, space x time, and recombine human history'' (491). This is a fantastic idea, typical of Ōe, that makes a fragment of truth a microcosm, encompassing or representing a totality in liminal space and time.

Contemporaneity treats liminality again and again as ''pure potency, where anything can happen, where immoderacy is normal, even normative, and where the elements of culture and society are released from their customary configurations and recombined in bizarre and terrifying imagery.''[39] Ōe's ''antistructural'' nation, which counters a differentiated, segmented society with its cultural constraints and social classifications, displays the potential for reevaluation and rethinking of the present, the essential function of communitas. Furthermore, in what Bakhtin calls the ''confrontation of times from the view of the present,''[40] popular laughter overpowers the hierarchical, official boundary of time and space.

This is when popular laughter becomes the pure potency of liminality that generates communitas. ''Laughter has the remarkable power of making an object come up close,'' Bakhtin states, ''of drawing it into a zone of crude contact where one can finger it familiarly on all sides, turn it upside down, inside out, peer at it from above and below, break open its external shell, look into its center, doubt it, take it apart, dismember it, lay it bare and expose it, examine it freely and experiment with it. Laughter demolishes fear and piety before an object, before a world . . . clearing the ground for an absolutely free investigation of it.''[41]

Out of this "ambivalent laughter" emerges the reality of a "lower" order, the concepts of the present, contemporary life, or contemporaneity. In his description of the "epic past" of the village=nation=minicosmos, Ōe parodies and lampoons the "absolute past" of the Great Empire of Japan; he lays it bare and turns it upside down; he "contemporizes" it, represents it "on a plane equal with contemporary life."[42] As the notion of cultural negation is central to the philosophical background of the village=nation=minicosmos, the concept of contemporaneity gives the novel its artistic framework.

Ōe, who is visually oriented, discovered the artistic representation of contemporaneity through his encounter with murals, a dominant form of graphic arts in Mexico.

> Three summers ago [1976] I went to Mexico, where I completed *The Pinch-runner Memorandum*. I came into contact with the Mexican Mural Movement, and met Octavio Paz and Garcia Márquez. It was quite a stimulus for me. Octavio Paz said that Mexico is a place where history is constantly bleeding. And there I found ancient times and the contemporary coexisting. Those colossal murals depict Mexican history from ancient times to the present synchronically. I said to myself, can it be done in literature? If you consider *The Game of Contemporaneity* as a mural, it portrays the history of a village from ancient times to the present. Right beneath the mural is a giant sprawling and looking at the entire history as contemporaneity. Both the writer and the reader can also read the novel in that fashion.[43]

Contemporaneity is specifically modeled after Diego Rivera's gigantic mural entitled, "Dream on a Sunday Afternoon in the Central Alameda" (1947–48), the central theme of which is "*calavera*" (skeleton).[44] In the series of mural scenes, Rivera presents a history of Mexico from Cortez to the present day. The mural is a panorama of Mexican history, the blood and sweat of the Mexican people, in which the past, present, and future coexist.

How does Ōe "contemporize" the panorama of the myth and history of the village=nation=minicosmos? How does he achieve the muralness that operates on the two principles of simultaneity and coexistence? Throughout the novel, Ōe visually stresses the existence and significance of *The One Who Destroys* by having the word set in dark, thick letter type.[45] It is as if the entire text of *Contemporaneity* were the virgin forest which the narrator was once instructed by *The One Who Destroys* to walk over in order to collect and assemble all the bones and minced flesh, to reconstruct the entirety of *The One Who Destroys*.

> My little sister, the meticulous instruction given to me in the long dream I saw had to do with the materiality of *The One Who Destroys* inside the forest. The gigantic body of *The One Who Destroys*, slaughtered and minced like meat that had just been quartered, was free of contamination and decomposition. The minced meat was buried in every inch of the forest with blood and marrow intact. . . . How could the feeble arms of a child carry the entire load of the giant's flesh? As I cringed in fear, I heard the words of encouragement. As a symbolic act, all I had to do was to walk over the places, without overlooking even a shred of muscle or joint, where the fragments of the flesh of *The One Who Destroys* were buried. (483)

So is the reader asked to follow and walk over the gigantic burial mound. He is to go through the text, the "forest of symbols,"[46] strewn with *The One Who Destroys* in thick, dark type as he reads the entirety of *Contemporaneity*, packed with the "flesh and spirit of the gigantic *The One Who Destroys*." Or, the reader is asked to join with the people on the last day of the Fifty-Day War "lying in tents put up in the lowest topos in the world framed by the masses of the gigantic trees," with the "soft ululation and high-sounding screech of the nocturnal forest as they contemplated the long, everlasting life of *The One Who Destroys*. It was as if they were, in anticipation of the annihilation of the village=nation=minicosmos, resurrecting a massive communal memory that went back to the Construction Period" (348). Standing right next to the narrator, the reader views with him a picture of the armed *The One Who Destroys* "lying among the gigantic trees in the virgin forest, an existence that combines individual soul and flesh for all the people of the village=nation=minicosmos" (348).

In search of liminal time and space, Ōe finally reaches the core of the forest (*mori*) that has appeared again and again in his previous works, sometimes Edenic, sometimes threatening, protective yet devouring, the womb and the grave at the same time. Symbolically he also combines the earlier hermaphrodite child image represented by Mori the idiot son with the trickster-cultural hero *The One Who Destroys*.[47] As readers of *Contemporaneity*, a narrative that reverberates with the rhythms of the primordial, primal generative power of the cosmos, we, like the ritual liminar, experience the intervening liminal period, which is likened to being in the womb, invisibility, darkness, and death. We wait with the narrator for the resurrection of *The One Who Destroys*, whom the twin sister has restored to ''a size as big as a dog.'' The novel is a gift to contemporary man who needs to recite a ''sacred'' narrative at the end of the ''ritual process'' that brings him into close rapport with the cosmic vision.

With B.A. degree and pen in hand, in February 1960 Ōe married Yukari, the oldest daughter of a film script writer, Itami Mansaku, whose son has been Ōe's friend since 1951. In May 1960 he traveled to the People's Republic of China as a member of the Japan-China Literary Delegation and met with Mao Zedong. (Four years later, in protest against the first nuclear test conducted by China, he resigned from the Association of Japan-China Cultural Exchange.) In 1961, he traveled through Eastern and Western Europe, including the Soviet Union, and met Sartre in Paris. In June 1963 his first boy, Hikari, was born with serious brain damage. Ōe put a stop to everything he was doing, visited Hiroshima in the summer, and in 1964 wrote *A Personal Matter*, which won the Shinchōsha Literary Prize. In spring 1965 he traveled to Okinawa, in the summer to the United States—in July and August to Harvard University; in September and October to Atlantic City and Hannibal, Missouri, Mark Twain's birthplace. He published another prize-winning novel (the Tanizaki Junichiro Prize), *The Football Game of the First Year of Manen*, in 1967, traveled to Australia and the United States in 1968, and toured Southeast Asia in 1970.

Between 1970 and 1973 he made a number of literary appearances which alternated with the publication of numerous essays and two stories. In 1973 he completed a two-volume novel, *The Waters Have Come in unto My Soul*, the Noma Literary Prize winner. His mentor, Professor Watanabe Kazuo, passed away in May 1975; in the same year Ōe joined a fourty-eight-hour hunger strike in protest of the persecution of Kim Chi Ha. In 1976 he taught for four months at Collegio de Mexico as a visiting professor. He spent exactly three years on each of his next two novels: *The Pinch-runner Memorandum*, published in 1976, and *The Game of Contemporaneity*, published in 1979. His narratives up to 1976 are collected in two six-volume editions; sixteen volumes of collected essays are devoted to contemporary issues and literature. In 1980, Ōe resumed writing short stories. In that year he published *A Collection of Modern Grotesque Stories* (Gendai denki shū). Two years later he published another collection of short stories, *Women Who Listen to "The Rain Tree"* ("Ame no ki" o kiku onnatachi). He calls his work, *Rouse up, O, Young Men of the New Age!* (Atarashii hito yo mezameyo), 1983, something of the "I-novel" (*shishōsetsu*). The book won the Osaragi Jirō Award. Now the father of three children, Ōe lives with his family in Seijō, Tokyo.

Notes

Notes to Chapter 1

1. Roland Barthes, "Introduction to the Structural Analysis of Narrative," *New Literary History* 6, 2 (Winter 1975):237.

2. A handful of his narratives, which have been translated into English, caught the immediate attention of American reviewers who have acclaimed him for his sophistication, obsessive brilliance, and enormous narrative power. "Oddly," Ann Redmon noted in her review of Ōe's *Teach Us to Outgrow Our Madness* (Warera no kyōki o ikinobiru michi o oshieyo, 1969), "his personal fixation never contaminates his art. In the vaunted creative process, he has transcended himself and given us an access to liberty." *London Times*, "This Story of Yours," October 15, 1978, sec. F, p. 40. Another enthusiastic review of the book comes from Ivan Gold: "Obsession in and of itself is hardly a guarantee of literary quality, but Ōe is a supremely gifted writer . . . able to 'fictionalize' the most significant elements of his life as can few others, and his work has enormous impact." "A Ray from the Rising Sun," *Washington Post*, September 11, 1977, sec. E, p. 4. Cornelia Holbert of *Best Sellers* wrote: "Ōe is a sophisticated and unerring writer, a great thinker and lover, not to be missed" (October 1977, p. 198). *Choice* called Ōe "a brilliantly obsessive writer" (December 1977, p. 1368). Of *A Personal Matter* (Kojinteki na taiken, 1964), Robert and Tomi Haas declared: "The publication of *A Personal Matter* marks the debut in English of an astonishing Japanese writer whose books deal with postwar youth with such uncompromising realism that he seems to have wrenched Japanese literature free of its deeply rooted, inbred tradition and moved it into the mainstream of world literature." *Saturday Review*, June 15, 1968, p. 31.

3. The novel tells of a man, Tokitō Kensaku, who agonizes over the adultery of his wife as he tries to overcome the torment and seeks self-salvation. The work has been translated into English by Edwin McClellan (New York: Kōdansha International, 1976).

4. "Fiction's Sorrow" (Shōsetsu no kanashimi), in *The Nuclear Conflagration and the Voice of "Man"* (Kaku no taika to "ningen" no koe) (Iwanami shoten, 1982), p. 239.

5. Ibid., p. 239. There are others, both novelists and critics, who have held Shiga responsible "for the stunting of modern Japanese fiction." See William F. Sibley, *The Shiga Hero* (Chicago: University of Chicago Press, 1979), pp. 1–2.

6. *Rabelais and His World*, trans. Helene Iswolsky (Cambridge: M.I.T. Press, 1968), p. 175. The emphasis is Bakhtin's. I discuss in detail the theory of "grotesque realism" in chapter 7.

7. *The Nuclear Conflagration*, p. 240.

8. Ibid., p. 236.

9. For the relationship between the "I-novel" and naturalism, see Janet A. Walker, *The Japanese Novel of the Meiji Period and the Ideal of Individualism* (Princeton: Princeton University Press, 1979), 4, particularly pp. 102–106. Also see William F. Sibley, "Naturalism in Japanese Literature," *Harvard Journal of Asiatic Studies* 28 (1968):157–69. In his "Akutagawa Ryunosuke and I-Novelists," Kinya Tsuruta analyzes the kind of definitions given by Japanese writers and critics. *Monumenta Nipponica* 25, 1–2 (1970):13–27. See also Noriko Mizuta Lippit, *Reality and Fiction in Modern Japanese Literature* (Armonk, N.Y.: M. E. Sharpe, 1980), pp. 13–38. Also see Edward Seidensticker, *This Country, Japan* (New York: Kodansha International, 1979), "The 'Pure' and the 'In-Between' in Modern Japanese Theories of the Novel." In this humorous 1966 article, Seidensticker traces the peculiar historical development of autobiographical fiction canonized by the "pure literature" of Shiga Naoya. The latest critical work on the "I-novel" is by Irmela Hijiya-Kirschnereit, *Selbstentblössungsrituale: Zur Theorie und Geschicte der autobiographischen Gattung "Shishösetsu" in der modernen Japanischen Literatur* (Franz Steiner Verlag, Germany: Wiesbaden, 1981). For further discussion on the "I-novel," see also chapter 4.

10. Masao Miyoshi, *Accomplices of Silence: The Modern Japanese Novel* (Berkeley: University of California Press, 1974), p. x. See also, pp. 72–74.

11. Ibid., p. xii.

12. Ibid.

13. See "From *A Personal Matter* to *The Pinch-runner Memorandum*" (*Kojinteki na taiken* kara *Pinchirannaa chōsho* made), in *Shinchō Contemporary Literature* (Shinchō gendai bungaku), vol. 55 (Shinchōsha, 1978), pp. 385–87. See also Sibley, *The Shiga Hero*, pp. 2–4.

14. *The Nuclear Conflagration*, p. 235.

15. "Linking the Novel and Reality" (Shōsetsu to genjitsu o musubu), in *The Nuclear Conflagration*, p. 110. As an example of contemporary literature, Ōe discusses the "various levels of reality" linked together in Günter Grass's *The Tin Drum*, which places German history in the contemporary world. This great novel, which hardly attracted the attention of Japanese scholars of German literature in Japan, has been duly "discovered" by Ōe, who wrote book reviews for a prestigious intellectual magazine, *Asahi Weekly* (Shūkan asahi), between 1965 and 1972. He was the first Japanese to review *The Tin Drum* and acclaim Grass for his achievement.

16. Thomas G. Winner, "Introduction" to Iu. M. Lotman's *Lectures on Structural Poetics, Theory in Verse*, Brown University Slavic Reprint V, 1968, p. ix. Ōe introduces Lotman's "art model theory" in *An Essay on Contemporary Age by Ōe Kenzaburo* (Ōe Kenzaburo dōjidaironshū), vol. 10 (Iwanami Shoten, 1981), pp. 49–51.

17. Quoted by Ann Shukman in *Literature and Semiotics: A Study of the Writings of Yu. M. Lotman* (New York: North-Holland Publishing Company, 1977), p. 50.

18. "Expressing the Expressive Life—My Moratorium 1" (Hyōgenseikatsu ni tsuite no hyōgen—waga moratoriamu 1), in *Ōe Kenzaburo zensakuhin* (Complete Works of Oe Kenzaburo, hereafter *OKZ*) (Shinchōsha). The first six volumes of *OKZ*, called series I, were published in 1966–67; the second six, called series II, in 1977–78. The quotation is from *OKZ*, vol. 2, series II, p. 201.

19. As if to challenge the literary world that denies authenticity and purity to "anything except the most personal of literature" (Seidensticker, "The 'Pure' and the 'In-Between,' " p. 101), Ōe published in 1983 what he calls his real *shishōsetsu*, *Rouse up, O, Young Men of the New Age* (Atarashii hito yo mezameyo), a collection of seven stories. The book won the Osaragi Jirō prize. Although Ōe takes up the format of the "I-novel," his latest stories again explore the power of imagination sparked by the words of his twenty-year-old son, Hikari, the poems of William Blake, and Ōe's own intellectual and emotional reminiscences. His *shishōsetsu* is radically different from the so-called pure literature and its egocentricity, which suggests "writers writing about writers for the sake of other writers," and "the *bundan*, the literary world, tight and cozy and turned in upon itself." See Seidensticker, "The 'Pure' and the 'In-Between,' "pp. 101 and 105.

20. "My Moratorium 1," *OKZ*, vol. 2, series II, pp. 219-20. The emphasis is mine.

21. Gaston Bachelard, *On Poetic Imagination and Reverie*, trans. Collette Gaudin (New York: Bobbs-Merrill, 1971), p. 19. The emphasis is Bachelard's.

22. Personal communication with the author.

23. An English translation by John Nathan is available in *Japan Quarterly* 12, 2 (1965):193-211.

24. A Japanese cultural anthropologist, Yamaguchi Masao, who brought Turner's theory to Ōe's attention, discusses "communitas," "liminality," "outsiderhood," and "structural inferiority" extensively in his *Culture and Ambivalence* (Bunka to ryōgisei) (Iwanami Shoten, 1975), pp. 229-35. Ōe mentions this anthropological connection between Turner and Yamaguchi in his discussion of José Guadalupe Posada [1851-1913] and Mexico: "I am reminded of a term by Turner, structural inferiority, which Yamaguchi Masao has further amplified." *The Method of a Novel* (Shōsetsu no hōhō) (Iwanami Gendai Sensho, 1978), p. 176.

25. Ōe loves to tell funny stories, which he has learned from the village "buffoon" and his mother. He used to tell funny stories to a group of young actors of the New Theatre who would loudly and indignantly call them a pack of lies. Ever since, Ōe tells us, his passion to tell funny stories has been considerably curbed. But, he asks, is there such a thing as an actor who lacks the imagination of a clown? "Clown Which Resists Terror" (Kyōfu ni sakarau dōke), *OKZ*, vol. 6, series II, p. 280.

26. Ibid., p. 281.

27. William Blake, quoted by Bachelard, *On Poetic Imagination*, p. 19.

28. There are several Japanese critics who deeply lament the suppression carried out by the Tokugawa Confucian regime and the censorship program of the Meiji government, which almost destroyed the aesthetics of laughter and of the trickster in Japanese literature. One such critic, Ikeda Hiroshi, writes that there was in the ruling samurai class a contemptuous attitude toward laughter, but also an awareness of its potential use as a subtle weapon by subordinate classes. Laughter was therefore considered extremely dangerous. See *Laughter in Japanese Literature* (Nihon bungaku no warai) (Wakō Sensho, 1977), p. 144. Hamada Yasuzō points out that laughter means liberation of sexuality and destroys the "sanctified code" of a rigid society, because all the participants in laughter are equal: "In no time other than the Meiji period had laughter in literature been so suppressed and exiled." See Hamada Yasuzō, comp., *Laughter: Sentiments and Beauty in Japanese Literature* (Warai—nihon bungaku ni okeru bi to jyōnen no nagare), (Gendai Shisōsha, 1973), pp. 340, 357-58. The most militant criticism comes from Iizawa Tadasu, who blames Tokugawa Confucianism for the destruction of critical spirit among the Japanese. The Japanese, he contends, are a people who have been forced to abandon laughter and satire: "Japan did possess a literature of laughter like European nations up until medieval times, then suddenly the

Tokugawa regime suppressed it, cutting off any chance for further growth." See *Laughter as a Weapon* (Buki to shite no warai) (Iwanami Shinsho, 1977), pp. 14, 22.

29. "Overcoming the Real World—My Moratorium 2" (Genjitsusekai no norikoe—waga moratoriamu 2), *OKZ*, vol. 3, series II, p. 264.

30. *Advertisements for Myself* (New York: G. P. Putnam's Sons, 1959),p. 271.

31. *Hiroshima Notes* (Hiroshima nōto) (Iwanami Shinsho, 1965), pp. 114–15.

32. The lecture, entitled "Japan's Search for Identity in the Nuclear Age," was given in December 1980. The quotations are based on a copy of the English translation of the lecture given to me by the author. The page numbers are from the revised version that appears in *The Nuclear Conflagration*.

33. Ibid., pp. 259–60.

34. Ibid., p. 264.

35. Kim Chi Ha, whose enormous talent has yet to be recognized in the West, has written many narrative poems. One, "The Tale of Mr. Shit" (Funji monogatari), treats bitingly and humorously the historical Japanese-Korean relationship. The title of the narrative poem is a parody of *The Tale of Genji* (*Genji monogatari*). Kim received a death sentence, later commuted to life imprisonment, for his critical comments on the Korean government. Some of Kim Chi Ha's works are available in English. *Chinogi* (a political drama), trans. Jean Inglis, Iwatani Kuniko, and Tsukahara Asako, with the collaboration of Chung Kyung-Mo, in *Ampo: Japan-Asia Quarterly Review* 2, 2–3 (1979):12–45; *Cry of the People and Other Poems* (Hayama, Japan: Autumn Press, 1974); *From the Darkness: Poems* (Kingston, R.I.: George Knowlton, 197?); *The Golden Crowned Jesus and Other writings*, ed. Chong Sun Kim and Shelly Killen (Maryknoll, N.Y.: Orbis Books, 1978); *The Middle Hour; Selected Poems of Kim Chi Ha*, trans. David R. McCann (Stanfordville, N.Y.: Human Rights Publishing Group, 1980); *Torture Road . . . 1974*, trans. Chong Sun Kim and Shelley Killen (Kingston, R.I.: George Knowlton, 1976).

36. "Japan's Search," pp. 280–81. The emphasis is Ōe's. His lifelong protests against nuclear weapons, suppression of human rights, and freedom of thought are due almost exclusively to his mentor, Professor Watanabe Kazuo, who exposed Ōe to French humanism at Tokyo University.

37. *Chicago Tribune*, June 22, 1969, p. 44. "Physicist, Purge Thyself," delivered to a meeting of the American Association of Physics Teachers, February 5, 1969.

38. *Palm Sunday* (New York: Delacorte Press, 1981), p. 70.

39. The lines are from W. H. Auden's poem, "Commentary," in *Journey to a War* (1939). He later revised the line, "The Voice of Man: O teach us to outgrow our madness" and changed it to "The human cry: O teach me to outgrow my madness" (London: Faber & Faber, 1973), rev. ed., p. 271.

40. *The Method of a Novel*, p. 9.

41. Tzvetan Todorov, *The Poetics of Prose*, trans. Richard Howard (Ithaca, N.Y.: Cornell University Press, 1977), p. 34.

42. *The Method of a Novel*, p. 9.

43. Todorov, *Poetics*, p. 25.

44. Gérard Genette, *Narrative Discourse: An Essay in Method*, trans. Jane E. Lewin (Ithaca, N.Y.: Cornell University Press, 1980), p. 27.

45. Todorov, "The Categories of Literary Narrative," *Papers on Language and Literature* (1980), p. 5.

46. "Reading Faulkner as a Writer" (Sakka to shite Fōkunaa o yomu), in *The Nuclear Conflagration*, p. 196.

47. Barthes, "The Structuralist Activity," in *Critical Theory since Plato*, ed. Hazard Adams (New York: Harcourt Brace Jovanovich, 1971), p. 1198.

48. *The Method of a Novel*, p. 11.

Notes to Chapter 2

1. *OKZ*, vol. 1, series I. All references to "Prize Stock" are John Nathan's translation in *Teach Us to Outgrow Our Madness* (New York: Grove Press, 1977).

2. Ōe later names this village Ōkubo village. It literally means "a big hollow" and becomes the background of a later work, *The Football Game of the First Year of Manen*. This same village reappears in his 1979 novel, *The Game of Contemporaneity*, with a different name.

3. "The Image System of Grotesque Realism" (Gurotesuku rearizumu no imēji shisutamu), *The Method of a Novel*, p. 194.

4. C. G. Jung and C. Kerényi, *Essays on a Science of Mythology*, trans. R. F. C. Hull (Princeton: Princeton University Press, 1969), p. 80.

5. "The Image System of Grotesque Realism," p. 197.

6. Ibid., p. 198. The other two elements of the "child archetype," invincibility and the child as beginning and end, represent the aesthetic world of "grotesque realism" in the image of the idiot son which Ōe takes up in his later works.

7. All references to *Nip the Buds* are from *OKZ*, vol. 1, series I.

8. Jung and Kerényi, p. 28.

9. "Linking the Novel and Reality," in *The Nuclear Conflagration*, p. 194.

10. Ibid., p. 105.

11. Oswald Ducrot and Tzvetan Todorov, *Encyclopedic Dictionary of the Sciences of Languange*, trans. Catherine Porter (Baltimore: The Johns Hopkins University Press, 1979), p. 263. The 1980 story, *The Trial*, appears in *A Collection of Modern Grotesque Stories* (Gendai denkishū) (Iwanami Gendai Sensho, 1980), pp. 137–270.

12. "Linking the Novel and Reality," in *The Nuclear Conflagration*, p. 106.

Notes to Chapter 3

1. "*Our Times* and Myself" (*Warera no jidai* to boku jishin), in *The Solemn Tightrope Walking* (Genshuku na tsunawatari) (Bungei Shunjū, 1965), p. 244. In 1956, Tanizaki Junichiro—the only other Japanese writer at this time to explore sexuality with fervor—wrote, at the age of seventy-three, his famous voyeuristic novel *The Key* (Kagi). And in this voyeurism lies the fundamental difference between Tanizaki's treatment of the sexual and Ōe's. The aged author reveled in a dark eroticism; the young novelist crusaded to demystify sex.

2. "Eccentricity, Abnormality, and Danger in Sex" (Sei no kikaisa to ijō to kiken), *Tightrope Walking*, p. 239.

3. "*Our Times* and Myself," p. 244.

4. "Sex in the Twentieth-Century Novel" (Nijusseiki shōsetsu no sei), *Tightrope Walking*, p. 261.

5. "Does Literature Have to Really Be Chosen?" (Hontō ni bungaku ga erabaren-eba naranai ka?), *OKZ*, vol. 1, series I, p. 368.

6. Ibid.

7. Ibid., p. 373.

8. Honda Shūgo, *A Narrative: The History of Postwar Literature* (Monogatari—sengo bungakushi) (Shinchōsha, 1966), pp. 751–90. There is a rather confused controversy over the existence and content of postwar literature. Some literary critics totally deny its significance by saying that postwar literature was actually "literature under the Occupation" (*senryōka no bungaku*) and contributed nothing new. See ibid. pp. 109–18. An article by another such critic, Etō Jun, was the cause of Honda's furious rebuttal concerning the validity of postwar literature: Etō calls postwar literature an "abortive flower" (*ada bana*) that bloomed under the political rule of the Occupation,

whereas Honda gives full credit to the efforts made by postwar writers to produce something new. Etō's article appears in *Asahi Shimbun*, evening edition, August 28 and 29, 1978, and Honda's response in September 2 and 3, 1978. Ōe also refutes Etō's argument in *Reading a Method* (Hōhō o yomu) (Kōdansha, 1980), pp. 7-30.

9. "How Did I Accept Postwar Literature?" (Sengobungaku o dō uketometa ka), *Tightrope Walking*, p. 186.

10. Ibid.

11. All references to *Our Times* are from *OKZ*, vol. 2, series I.

12. Supplement no. 3 to *OKZ*, vol. 2, series I, p. 16.

13. All references to "Sheep" are from *OKZ*, vol. 1, series I. Translated by Frank T. Motofuji, *Japan Quarterly* 17, 2 (1970):167-77. I have slightly altered his translation.

14. All references to "Leap Before You Look" are from *OKZ*, vol. 1, series I. The title of the story comes from W. H. Auden's poem by the same title. The first stanza goes: "The sense of danger must not disappear:/The way is certainly both short and steep,/However gradual it looks from here;/Look if you like, but you will have to leap." *Collected Shorter Poems 1927-1957* (New York: Vintage Books, 1975), p. 200.

15. The story appears in 5OKZ, vol. 2, series I, pp. 5-22.

16. The story appears in *OKZ*, vol. 2, series I, pp. 51-80.

17. Structurally, *Our Times* is a mixture of NOW and THEN, what is occurring now and remembrances, alternating one chapter of the X-Y story with that of the three young men in and out of trouble.

18. Toward the end of the story we realize the reason for the inclusion of the trio's story in *Our Times*: 1) thematically, the obsessive yearning for the purchase of a large truck by the trio, the desire for mobility, is a reflection of the closed world of the postwar generation represented by Yasuo; 2) in terms of plot, the erosion of their comradeship and Yasuo's subsequent rescue efforts for Shigeru lead to the disclosure of the Yasuo-Arab alliance, and ultimately to the dissolution of Yasuo's only way out, the escape to France.

19. X becomes the hero who is not given any prohibition to violate, or a forbidden boundary which he must cross in the "closed vs. open" opposition that is an essential feature of the spatial structure of a story. According to Lotman's theory, Ōe's stories are "plotless," because "the movement of the plot, the event, is the crossing of that forbidden border which the plotless structure establishes." In terms of "artistic space," when the hero merely moves *within* the space assigned to him it cannot be called an event. An event becomes a plot only when the hero crosses "the basic topological border in the plot's spatial structure." Lotman, *The Structure of the Artistic Text*, trans. Ronald Vroon, Michigan Slavic Contributions, No. 7 (Ann Arbor: University of Michigan, 1977), p. 238. The emphasis is Lotman's.

Notes to Chapter 4

1. *OKZ*, vol. 2, series I, p. 351.

2. Mark Twain, *The Adventures of Huckleberry Finn* (New York: W. W. Norton,1977), p. 169.

3. Ibid., p. 170.

4. *OKZ*, vol. 2, series I, pp. 353-54.

5. Ibid., p. 366.

6. The term is used by Richard Poirier in his *Norman Mailer* (New York: Viking, 1972), p. 6.

7. See Robert Alter's *Rogue's Progress: Studies in the Picaresque Novel*

(Cambridge: Harvard University Press, 1964), pp. 117–21, and Barbara A. Babcock's "Liberty's a Whore," in *The Reversible World: Symbolic Inversion in Art and Society*, ed. Barbara A. Babcock (Ithaca: Cornell University Press, 1978), p. 102.

8. Robert B. Heilman, "Variations on Picaresque (Felix Krull)," *Sewanee Review* 66 (1958):556.

9. All references to *The Youth* are from *OKZ*, vol. 4, series I.

10. See Heilman, "Variations on Picaresque," p. 548; Babcock, "Liberty's a Whore," p. 97; Ulrich Wicks, "The Nature of Picaresque Narrative," *PMLA* 89 (1974):244.

11. Heilman, "Variations on Picaresque," p. 562.

12. Wicks, "Picaresque Narrative," p. 245.

13. W. M. Frohock, "The Idea of the Picaresque," *Yearbook of Comparative and General Literature* 16 (1967): p. 45.

14. Ibid.

15. Edith Kern, "Introduction," in *Sartre*, ed. Edith Kern (Englewood Cliffs, N.J.: Prentice-Hall, 1962), p. 14.

16. All references to *Outcries* are from *OKZ*, vol. 5, series I.

17. Kern, "Introduction," p. 11.

18. H. J. Blackham, "Anguished Responsibility," in *Sartre*, p. 166.

19. Ōe closely follows the actual case from the Korean boy's encounter with a high school girl, the murder, to the trial.

20. Jean-Paul Sartre, quoted by Blackham, "Anguished Responsibility," p. 169.

21. Heilman, "Variations on Picaresque," p. 565.

22. Ibid., p. 564.

23. All references to *Everyday Life* are from *OKZ*, vol. 5, series I.

24. Wicks, "Picaresque Narrative," p. 244.

25. Heilman, "Variations on Picaresque," p. 564.

26. Frohock, "Idea of Picaresque," p. 45.

27. Miyoshi, *Accomplices of Silence*, p. 73. Also, see Sibley, pp. 2–4.

28. See chapter 6.

29. Babcock, "Liberty's a Whore," p. 104.

30. Alter, *Rogue's Progress*, pp. 119–20.

Notes to Chapter 5

1. Roland Barthes, "Structural Analysis," p. 243.

2. "The Football of Simultaneity" (Dōjisei no futtoboru), *The Enduring Volition* (Jizokusuru kokorozashi) (Bungei Shunjū, 1968), p. 403.

3. Ibid., p. 408.

4. All references to *Manen* are my translation. *OKZ*, vol. 1, series II. The second number in the bracket after each quotation indicates an English translation entitled *The Silent Cry*, by John Bester (New York: Kōdansha International, 1974).

5. Mitsusaburo and Takashi are the third and fourth sons of the Nedokoros; the first and second sons are dead. Nedokoro means "a place of roots."

6. Genette, *Narrative Discourse*, p. 162.

7. "The Football of Simultaneity," p. 408.

8. See chapter 2 for discussion of the two stories.

9. He takes it up again in *The Trial of "Nip the Buds, Gun the Kids."*

Notes to Chapter 6

1. In his "García Márquez: The Uses of Repetition" (to appear in *Anthol-*

ogy of Critical Essays on García Márquez), Alfred MacAdam points out that García Márquez's stories, which rely on the same use of repetition, present the literary critic with a difficult task because repetition "does not occur within but between texts . . . an incident may be a short story or an element in a novella, either a piece or a whole, with only superficial changes." He suggests that the repetitions might be compared to the cinematic technique of "takes." In other words, a repeated incident or a paragraph functions like different versions of a shot, as each shot corresponds with a part of the director's complex vision of a scene.

2. *Selected Poetry and Prose of William Blake*, ed. Northrop Frye (New York: Modern Library, 1953), p. 27.

3. All references to "Father" are from *OKZ*, vol. 3, series II.

4. Todorov, *The Poetics of Prose*. p. 145.

5. *William Blake*, ed. Northrop Frye, p. 27.

6. *OKZ*, vol. 3, series II. All references to *My Tears* are John Nathan's translation in *Teach Us*.

7. *OKZ*, vol. 3, series II. All references to "Teach Us" are John Nathan's translation in *Teach Us*.

8. Genette, *Narrative Discourse*, p. 116.

9. *Russian Formalist Criticism: Four Essays*, trans. Lee T. Lemon and Marion J. Reis (Lincoln: University of Nebraska Press, 1965), p. 95.

10. Genette, *Narrative Discourse*, pp. 113-60.

11. Barthes, *S/Z*, trans. Richard Miller (New York: Hill and Wang, 1974), p. 32.

12. Genette, *Narrative Discourse*, p. 172.

13. Ibid., p. 174.

14. Ibid., p. 170.

15. The Japanese language does not require personal pronouns in conversations because a verb form assumes the relationship of the speaker and the listener and also distinguishes masculine speech from feminine by the use of different verbal endings.

16. MacAdam, *Modern Latin American Naratives: The Dreams of Reason* (Chicago: University of Chicago Press, 1977), p. 79.

17. Julia Kristeva, *Desire in Language: A Semiotic Approach to Literature and Art*, trans. Thomas Gora, Alice Jardine, and Leon S. Roudiez (New York: Columbia University Press, 1980), p. 69.

18. *Volunteering for Parody* (Parodi shigan) (Chūō Kōronsha, 1979), pp. 39 and 42.

19. O. M. Friedenberg, "The Origin of Paraody," *Semiotics and Structuralism*, ed. H. Baran (White Plains: International Arts and Sciences Press, 1974), p. 278. I have come across *Discussions on Ōe Kenzaburo* (Ōe Kenzaburo ron) by Hasumi Shigehiko (Seidosha, 1980), the only Japanexe book I have seen that analyzes Ōe's narratives from a numerical/semiotic perspective and with a delightful sense of humor.

21. Ōe talks extensively about this device in *The Method of a Novel*, pp. 2-5. The translation is by Ann Shukman, *Literature and Semiotics*, pp. 41-42. Also, see Lemon, *Russian Formalist Critics*, p. 12.

22. Ōe wrote: "There has been a tendency in the modern/contemporary novels of our country to be concerned with the similitude of the situations described in the novels with those of everyday life. Under these circumstances, criticism that the wooden horse Don Quixote and Sancho Panza ride is incapable of flying can even exist; or criticism that Don Quixote's cosmology violates basic scientific premises, and that it is inconceivable for Sancho Panza to view the heavens from the back of the wooden horse fixed on the ground, can hold water. Suffice it to say that in our current literary criticism, the approach that examines situations in the novel for their similarity to those of everyday life is still alive and strong." *The Method of a Novel*, pp. 159-60.

23. "Can a Writer Remain Absolutely Antipolitical?" (Sakka wa zettai ni hanseiji-teki tariru ka?), *OKZ*, vol. 3, series I, p. 382. Originally, Ōe wrote a companion story, "The Moon Man" (Tsuki no otoko, 1972), to *My Tears*. In this allegorical story he tackles the concept of "the pure Emperor" (junsui tennō) in the space age.

24. Ibid., p. 383.

25. (Kōdansha, 1973), p. 296.

26. Ibid., pp. 304-305. The emphasis is Ōe's.

27. Regina Janes, *Gabriel García Márquez: Revolutions in Wonderland* (Columbia: University of Missouri Press, 1981), p. 245.

28. "Can a Writer Remain Absolutely Antipolitical?," p. 382.

Notes to Chapter 7

1. I shall discuss the concept of "grotesque realism" in detail in a later section.

2. Todorov, *The Poetics of Prose*, p. 244.

3. Ibid., p. 245. These terms are drawn from modern linguistics and applied extensively by the structuralists. For example, Saussure's main concern in studying a language was that of "relationships of identities and differences." Jonathan Culler writes that

> On the one hand, there are those . . . oppositions which produce distinct and alternative terms. . . . On the other hand, there are the relations between units which combine to form sequences. In a linguistic sequence, a term's value depends not only on the contrast between it and the others which might have been chosen in its stead but also on its relations with the terms which precede and follow it in sequence. The former, which Saussure calls *associative* relations, are now generally called paradigmatic relations. The latter are called *syntagmatic* relations. Syntagmatic relations define combinatory possibilities: the relations between elements which combine in a sequence. Paradigmatic relations are the oppositions between elements which replace one another.

Ferdinand de Saussure (New York: Penguin, 1977), pp. 44-45. Also see Roland Barthes, *Elements of Semiology*, trans. Annette Lavers and Colin Smith (New York: Hill and Wang, 1979), pp. 58-59. Todorov and Ducrot explain the term "syntagm" or "syntagmatic relationship" in their *Encyclopedic Dictionary of the Sciences of Language*, pp. 106-108. Ōe wrote in 1958 a series of works that show a good paradigmatic relation. Throughout the four stories ("Leap Before You Look," "A Dark River, Heavy Oars," "Cheers," and *Our Times*), the protagonist undergoes absolutely no psychological development or spiritual growth. Ōe could have used four variations of a theme in which the protagonist would go from one dramatic experience to another, mature progressively from one disequilibrium to another, all the stories combined in a sequential development. In other words, the four stories would have a "syntagmatic" relationship. Instead, they cancel each other out. Story A is replaced by Story B, Story B by Story C, and so on. The result is that there is no reciprocal or "syntagmatic" relationship among them. The triangular relationship of XYZ is a paradigm for Ōe that provides several combinatory possibilities of XYZ. His "paradigmatic" use of the stories describes the kind of literary universe the novelist has grappled with in his pre-1964 works.

4. *The Poetics of Prose*, p. 245.

5. All references to "Agwhee" are from *OKZ*, vol. 6, series II. Translated by John Nathan in *Teach Us*.

6. All references to *A Personal Matter* are from *OKZ*, vol. 6, series II. Translated by John Nathan (New York: Grove Press, 1968).

7. Mikhail M. Bakhtin, *Problems of Dostoevsky's Poetics*, trans. R. W. Rotsel (Ann Arbor: Ardis, 1977), p. 38.

8. Ibid.

9. All references to "Teach Us" are from *OKZ*, vol. 3, series II. Translated by John Nathan.

10. Watanabe Hiroshi speculates that the name Jin possibly comes from the German word *Sinn*, meaning "sense," and is probably used synonymously with the word "subconscious." Supplement to *OKZ*, vol. 4, series II, p. 5.

11. All references to *The Waters* are from *OKZ*, vol. 4, series II.

12. According to Saussure, "*La langue* is the system of a language, the language as a system of forms, whereas *parole* is actual speech, the speech acts that are made possible by the language. . . . *Parole* . . . is the 'executive side of language,' and for Saussure," Culler writes, "involves both 'combinations by which the speaker uses the code of the linguistic system in order to express his own thoughts' and 'the psycho-physical mechanisms which permit him to externalize these combinations.'" *Saussure*, pp. 22–23. Ōe's hero, Mori (or Jin), unable to recognize the existence of *langue* and *parole*, provides Ōe with a fundamental question of *kotoba* (langue), and its function as *kōjutsu* (parole), the very basis of *shōsetsu*, or narratives, which he strongly feels should be the main interest of literary criticism, not the sentimental evaluation of a writer's personal life and emotions (*jinseironteki kankai*). See his *The Method of a Novel*, p. 22.

13. I am indebted to Todorov's discussion on the genre of the fantastic. *The Fantastic: A Structural Approach to a Literary Genre*, trans. Richard Howard (Ithaca: Cornell University Press, 1975), especially see pp. 107–23.

14. Todorov, *The Fantastic*, ibid., p. 113.

15. Ibid., p. 83.

16. All references to *The Pinch-runner* are from *OKZ*, vol. 6, series II.

17. Todorov, *The Fantastic*, p. 20.

18. Ōe also employs this structure in *The Day He Himself Shall Wipe My Tears Away*. See chapter 6.

19. Todorov discusses similar characteristics of madness, drug experiences, and the world of infancy, all of which share an averbal universe and the dissolution of the psychic and physical world. See *The Fantastic*, pp. 115–16.

20. See *The Fantastic*, pp. 38–39. The term refers to those words commonly called "auxiliaries" such as *may*, *might*, *should*, together with adverbs like *probably*, *perhaps*, and *maybe*. The emphasis in the following quotation is mine.

21. In "Toward the Imagination of Buffoonery and Regeneration," Ōe brilliantly traces the elements of "grotesque realism" and the Winnebago Indians' trickster figure in *Fire on the Plain* (Nobi) by Ōoka Shohei and *The Sufferer* (Kataku no hito) by Dan Kazuo. *Via Words: Situations and Literature* (Kotoba ni yotte—jōkyō to bungaku) (Shinchōsha, 1976), pp. 263–89. Also see Bakhtin, *Rabelais*, pp. 19–20.

22. Watanabe Hiroshi in Supplement to *OKZ*, vol. 6, series II, p. 2.

23. Matthew Hodgart, *Satire* (New York: McGraw-Hill, World University Library, 1973), p. 10.

24. See Bakhtin, *Rabelais*, pp. 78–79.

25. Hodgart, *Satire*, p. 23.

26. Ibid., p. 11.

27. Elder Olson, *The Theory of Comedy* (Bloomington: Indiana University Press, 1975), p. 58.

28. Olson (pp. 5 and 61) points out the comic response which depends upon three

conditions: 1) the kind of person laughed at (what is laughed at); 2) the frame of mind of the laughter (who does the laughing); 3) the particular cause of the laughter (relation betwen the object of laughter and the subject who laughs).

29. Hodgart, *Satire*, p. 12.

30. *Iwana* (*Salvelinus pluvius*) belongs to the Charrs family, a kind of brook trout. Along with the fish called *yamame* (*Onchorhynchus masou*), this fish is used as a metaphor which embodies the ideal collectivity of the human race.

31. Paul Radin, *The Trickster* (New York: Greenwood Press, 1975), p. 133. See chapter 8 for Ōe's full treatment of the trickster figure.

32. Ibid., p. ix.

33. Bakhtin, *Rabelais*, p. 24.

34. In "Commentary" by Yamaguchi Masao to the Japanese translation of Radin's *The Trickster*. Quoted by Ōe in *The Method of a Novel*, p. 134.

Notes to Chapter 8

1. All references to *The Game of Contemporaneity* are from the Shinchōsha edition, 1979.

2. Barbara Babcock-Abrahams, " 'A Tolerated Margin of Mess': The Trickster and His Tales Reconsidered," *Journal of the Folklore Institute* 17, 3 (1975):148.

3. Ibid., p. 158.

4. "One Hour with Ōe Kenzaburo-san" (Ōe Kenzaburo-san to ichijikan) *Asahi Shimbun*, August 15, 1979. The emphasis is mine.

5. Victor Turner, *Dramas, Fields, and Metaphors* (Ithaca: Cornell University Press, 1974), p. 231.

6. Victor Turner, *The Ritual Process: Structure and Anti-Structure* (Ithaca: Cornell University Press, 1969), p. 95.

7. Turner, *Dramas*, p. 232.

8. Turner, *The Ritual Process*, p. 96.

9. Ibid.

10. Ibid.

11. Ibid., p. 124.

12. Turner, *Dramas*, p. 233.

13. For the details, see *New York Times*, July 18, 1975, p. 4.

14. *The Method of a Novel*, p. 183.

15. Ibid., pp. 182–85.

16. Ibid., p. 184.

17. See Ienaga Saburo's *The Pacific War 1931–1945*, trans. Frank Baldwin (New York: Pantheon Books, 1978), pp. 97–128, for the actual restriction of freedom of thought and speech imposed by the Japanese government.

18. Ienaga writes: "In 1943 the Special Law on Wartime Crimes, enacted only a year before, was revised to include the interfering with government administration: 'To disseminate information during wartime which will harm public order for the purpose of interfering with national administration or public order' became a crime." Ibid., p. 99.

19. Turner, *Dramas*, p. 232.

20. For example, Ōe introduces an expression, *otobiagari ga*, in connection with the "baseball odyssey" of the narrator's youngest brother, Tsuyutome-san, a promising pitcher, and his manager/protector, Kōniichan. An "imaginative fish dealer," Kōniichan was also a clown. One day he was walking by the stationer's where an unmarried female schoolteacher was taking care of the store. As soon as he saw her sitting there, he jumped straight up. An unusually large man, he hit his head on the

lintel and fell unconscious to the dirt floor. When asked by the father what had happened, the schoolteacher simply said, "rule——He leapt!" (*Otobiagaritan desu ga*) (378). Kōnii-chan and Tsuyutome-san travel all over Japan in search of the right kind of baseball team for Tsuyutome-san. Kōniichan keeps sending telegrams to his father: "TSUYU-TOME GOOD CHANCE TO BE HIRED BY GIANTS," "HANSHIN OR TOKYO, TSUYUTOME STILL DEBATING," "FINALLY TSUYUTOME DECIDED TO JOIN DRAGONS NEGOTIATIONS WITH COACH COMMENCED WAIT FOR GOOD NEWS." However, no good news arrives: "Since his father could not stand the mailman's ridicule, he made an arrangement with the postmaster to pick up the telegrams once a week. ——That timber topper! [*otobiagari ga*] the father popped his cork, and the epithet, 'timber topper,' became the standard derisive expression in our land that refers to someone like Kōniichan who is easily elated" (397).

21. *Asahi Shimbun*, August 15, 1979.

22. The narrator sees in his mind's eye "a ship going upstream in the pitch-black darkness, a reed boat which transported the deformed baby Hiruko into the 'marginal' world" (41). Ōe also talks about Hiruko with respect to marginality and grotesque realism in *The Method of a Novel*, p. 175. See also Michael Czaja's *Gods of Myth and Stone* (Tokyo: Weatherhill, 1974), pp. 148, 207.

23. Michel Foucault, *Madness and Civilization: A History of Insanity in the Age of Reason*, trans. Richard Howard (New York: Vintage Books, 1973), p. 9.

24. The emphasis is mine.

25. Turner, "Frame, Flow and Reflection: Ritual and Drama as Public Limi-nality," *Japanese Journal of Religious Studies* 6, 4 (December 1979):465. Barbara G. Myerhoff also points out that "backwardness" or reversals in the rituals of the Huichol Indians of North-Central Mexico reveal the essential attitude of the sacred, the reestablishment of the primordial condition of man and the concretization of the ineffable. See "Return to Wirikuta: Ritual Reversal and Symbolic Continuity on the Peyote Hunt of the Huichol Indians" in *The Reversible World: Symbolic Inversion in Art and Society*, ed. Barbara A. Babcock (Ithaca: Cornell University Press, 1978), pp. 225–39.

26. Ōe sometimes writes sentences that do not have the usual "subject + verb" construction. Instead of saying ". . . mizu no michi o tadoritsuzukeru koto de, gaibusekai kara no koritsu o hukametsutsu, sokō o okonatta" (. . . they went upstream through the waterway, intensifying their solitude from the outer world), Ōe completes the sentence with a noun phrase: ". . . karera ga okonatta sokō." This style enhances the poeticalness of the narration.

27. Laura Makarius, "Ritual Clowns and Symbolic Behavior," *Diogenes* 69 (1970):46.

28. See Makarius, Babcock-Abrahams, and Turner's "Myth and Symbol," in *International Encyclopedia of the Social Sciences*, 1968 ed.

29. The narrator superimposes the image of the "immortal Stalin" upon that of *The One Who Destroys*. See pp. 152–53.

30. Makarius, "Ritual Clowns," p. 52.

31. A mushroom, another variation of the jar-keyhole shape, is what *The One Who Destroys* transforms into after its latest death.

32. Czaja, *Gods of Myth and Stone*, pp. 28-27.

33. Makarius, "Ritual Clowns," p. 58.

34. Turner, *The Ritual Process*, p. 45.

35. Ibid., p. 49.

36. Turner, "Myth and Symbol."

37. *The Dialogic Imagination*, trans. Caryl Emerson and Michael Holquist (Austin: University of Texas Press, 1981), p. 21.

38. Turner, *Dramas*, p. 255.
39. Turner, "Myth and Symbol."
40. Bakhtin, *The Dialogic Imagination*, p. 26.
41. Ibid., p. 23.
42. Ibid., p. 21.
43. *Asahi Shimbun*.
44. See *The Method of a Novel*, p. 170.
45. Ōe employs the same technique in *The Day He Himself Shall Wipe My Tears Away* with the word *ano hito*, "The Man."
46. The phrase is one of Turner's book titles (Ithaca: Cornell University Press, 1967).
47. See chapter 7.

Selected Bibliography

Unless otherwise indicated, Ōe's narratives are included in *Ōe Kenzaburo zensakuhin* (Complete Works of Ōe Kenzaburo), Series I and II. Shinchōsha, 1966–1978. The place of publication for books in Japanese is Tokyo.

1957   "Kimyōna shigoto" (A Strange Job).
      "Lavish Are the Dead" (Shisha no ogori). Translated by John Nathan. *Japan Quarterly* 12, 2 (1965):193–211.
      "Someone Else's Feet" (Tanin no ashi). Translated by Ruth W. Adler. *Bulletin of Concerned Asian Scholars* 14, 2 (1982):55–61.
      "Gishō no toki" (The False Testimony).
1958   "Prize Stock" (Shiiku). Translated by John Nathan. In *Teach Us to Outgrow Our Madness*. New York: Grove Press, 1977, pp. 111–68.
      "Sheep" (Ningen no hitsuji). Translated by Frank T. Motofuji. *Japan Quarterly* 17, 2 (1970): 167–77.
      "Unpan" (A Haul).
      Memushiri kouchi (Nip the Buds, Gun the Kids).
      "Miru mae ni tobe" (Leap Before You Look).
      Kurai kawa omoi kai" (A Dark River, Heavy Oars).
      "Tori" (Birds).
      "Fui no oshi" (A Mute).
      "Kassai" (Cheers).
      "Tatakai no kyō" (Today the Struggle).
1959   *Warera no jidai* (Our Times).
      "Koko yori hoka no basho" (Another Place).
      "Kyōdō seikatsu" (Collective Life).
      Seinen no omei (The Young Man's Stigma).
      "Jōkigen" (In Excellent Humor).
1960   "Yūkan na heishi no otōto" (A Brave Soldier's Kid Brother).
      "Kakō seikatsusha" (A Down-and-Out Person).
      "Kōtai seinen kenkyūjo" (A Research Center for Degenerate Youth).
1961   "Kōfuku na wakai giriaku-jin" (A Young Happy Gilyak).
      "Sebunteen" (Seventeen).
      "Seiji Shōnen shisu" (A Political Boy Is Now Dead). Unavailable.

"Fumanzoku" (Discontent).
1962 *Okurete kita seinen* (A Youth Who Came in Late).
Sakebigoe (Outcries).
1963 "Suparuta kyōiku" (The Spartan Education).
"Seiteki ningen" (Homo Sexualis).
"Keirō shūkan" (The Week for the Aged).
1964 "Atomikku ēgi no shugojin" (A Guardian of the Atomic Age).
Nichijōseikatsu no bōken (Adventures of Everyday Life).
"Aghwee the Sky Monster" (Sora no kaibutsu aguwee). Translated by John Nathan. In *Teach Us to Outgrow Our Madness*. New York: Grove Press, 1977, pp. 221-61.
"Burajirufū no porutogarugo" (The Brazilian Portuguese).
"Inu no sekai" (Dogs' World).
A Personal Matter (Kojinteki na taiken). Translated by John Nathan. New York: Grove Press, 1968.
1965 *Genshuku na tsunawatari* (The Solemn Tightrope Walking). Bungei shunjū.
Hiroshima nōto (Hiroshima Notes). Iwanami Shinsho.
1967 *The Silent Cry* (Manengannen no fottoboru). Translated by John Bester. New York: Kōdansha International, 1974.
"Hashire, hashire tsuzukeyo" (Run, Keep on Running).
1968 "Ikenie otoko wa hitsuyō ka" (Is a Sacrificial Man Necessary?).
"Shuryō de kurashita warera no senzo" (Our Hunting Fathers).
"Kakujidai no mori no intonsha" (The Hermit of the Forest in the Nuclear Age).
"Chichi yo anata wa doko e ikuno ka?" (Father, Where Are You Going?).
Jizokusuru kokorozashi (Enduring Volition). Bungei shunjū.
1969 "Teach Us to Outgrow Our Madness" (Warera no kyōki o ikinobiru michi o oshieyo). Translated by John Nathan. In *Teach Us to Outgrow Our Madness*. New York: Grove Press, 1977, pp. 169-219.
1970 *Okinawa Nōto* (Okinawa Notes). Iwanami Shinsho.
Kowaremono to shite no ningen (Fragile Human). Kōdansha.
Kakujidai no sōzōryoku (The Imagination of the Nuclear Age). Shinchō Sensho.
1971 *The Day He Himself Shall Wipe My Tears Away* (Mizu kara waga namida o nuguitamoo hi). Translated by John Nathan. In *Teach Us to Outgrow Our Madness*. New York: Grove Press, 1977, pp. 1-110.
Genbakugo no ningen (Homo Sapien after the A-Bomb). Shinchō Sensho.
1972 *The Day the Whales Shall Be Annihilated* (Kujira no shimetsu suru hi). Bungei Shunjū.
1973 *Kōzui wa waga tamashii ni oyobi* (The Waters Have Come in unto My Soul).
Dōjidai to shite no sengo (Postwar as the Contemporaneity).
1974 *Jyōkyō e* (Toward Situations). Iwanami Shoten.
Bungaku Nōto (Literary Notes). Shinchōsa.
1976 *Pinchiranna chosho* (The Pinch-runner Memorandum).
Kotoba ni yotte: Jyōkō/bungaku (Via Words: Situations/Literature). Shinchōsha.
1978 *Shōsetsu no hōhō* (The Method of a Novel). Iwanami Gendai Sensho.
1979 *Dōjidai gēmu* (The Game of Contemporaneity). Shinchōsha. Excerpts trans. Michiko N. Wilson. *O.ARS: B* (1983): 141-43.
1980 *Gendai denkishū* (A Collection of Modern Grotesque Stories). Iwanami Gendai Sensho.
1981 *Ōe Kenzaburo dōjidaironshū* (An Essay on Contemporary Age by Ōe Kenzaburo). 10 vols. Iwanami Shoten.
1982 *Kaku no taika to "ningen" no koe* (The Nuclear Conflagration and the Voice of "Man"). Iwanami Shoten.
"*Ame no ki*" *o kiku onnatachi* (Women Who Listen to the "Rain Tree"). Shinchōsha.
1983 *Atarashii hito yo mezameyo* (O, Rouse up, Young Men of the New Age). Kōdansha.
1984 *Ika ni ki o korosu ka* (How to Kill a Tree). Bungei Shunjū.

Alter, Robert. *Rogue's Progress: Studies in the Picaresque Novel*. Cambridge: Harvard University Press, 1964.

Auden, W. H. *Collected Shorter Poems 1927-1957*. New York: Vintage Books, 1975.

Babcock, Barbara A. " 'Liberty's a Whore': Inversions, Marginalia, and Picaresque Narrative." In *The Reversible World: Symbolic Inversions in Art and Society.* Edited by Barbara A. Babcock. Ithaca: Cornell University Press, 1978, pp. 93—116.

————— " 'A Tolerated Margin of Mess': The Trickster and His Tales Reconsidered." *Journal of the Folklore Institute* 17, 3 (1975):147-86.

Bachelard, Gaston. *On Poetic Imagination and Reverie.* Translated by Colette Gaudin. New York: Bobbs-Merrill, 1971.

Bakhtin, Mikhail M. *Problems of Dostoevsky's Poetics.* Translated by R. W. Rotsel. Ann Arbor: Ardis, 1977.

————— *Rabelais and His World.* Translated by Helen Iswolsky. Cambridge: The Massachusetts Institute of Technology Press, 1968.

————— *The Dialogic Imagination.* Translated by Caryl Emerson and Michael Holquist. Austin: University of Texas Press, 1981.

Baran, Henryk, ed. *Semiotics and Structuralism.* Translated by H. Baran, A. J. Hollander, and William Mandel. White Plains, N.Y.: International Arts and Science Press, 1974.

Barthes, Roland. *Elements of Semiology.* Translated by Annette Lavers and Colin Smith. New York: Hill and Wang, 1979.

————— "Introduction to the Structural Analysis of Narrative." *New Literary History* 6, 2 (Winter 1975):237-72.

————— "The Structuralist Activity." In *Critical Theory Since Plato.* Edited by Hazard Adams. New York: Harcourt Brace Jovanovich, 1971, pp. 1196-99.

————— *S/Z.* Translated by Richard Miller. New York: Hill and Wang, 1974.

Blake, William. *Selected Poetry and Prose of William Blake.* Edited by Northrop Frye. New York: Modern Library, 1953.

Blackham, H. J. "Anguished Responsibility." In *Sartre.* Edited by Edith Kern. Englewood Cliffs, N.J.: Prentice-Hall, 1962, pp. 166-71.

Culler, Jonathan. *Ferdinand de Saussure.* New York: Penguin, 1977.

Czaja, Michael. *Gods of Myth and Stone.* Tokyo: Weatherhill, 1974.

Ducrot, Osland and Tzvetan Todorov. *Encyclopedic Dictionary of the Sciences of Language.* Translated by Catherine Porter. Baltimore: The Johns Hopkins University Press, 1979.

Foucault, Michel. *Madness and Civilization: A History of Insanity in the Age of Reason.* Translated by Richard Howard. New York: Vintage Books, 1973.

Friedenberg, O. M. "The Origin of Parody." In *Semiotics and Structuralism.* Edited by Henryk Baran. White Plains, N.Y.: International Arts and Sciences Press, 1974, pp. 269-83.

Frohock, W. M. "The Idea of the Picaresque." In *Yearbook of Comparative and General Literature* 16 (1967):43-52.

Genett, Gérard. *Narrative Discourse: An Essay in Method.* Translated by Jane E. Lewin. Ithaca: Cornell University Press, 1980.

Grass, Günter. *The Tin Drum.* Translated by Ralph Manheim. New York: Vintage Books, 1964.

Hamada Yasuzō, comp. *Warai—nihon bungaku ni okeru bi to jyōnen no nagare* (Laughter: Sentiments and Beauty in Japanese Literature). Gendai Shisōsha, 1973.

Harbison, Mark A. Review of *O Rouse up, Young Men of the New Age*, by Ōe Kenzaburo. *Japan Book News*, October 1, 1984, p. 29.

Heilman, Robert B. "Variations on Picaresque (Felix Krull)." *Sewanee Review* 66 (1958):547-77.

Hijiya-Kirschnereit, Irmela. *Selbstentblössungsrituale: Zur Theorie und Geschichte der autobiographischen Gattung "Shishōsetsu" in der modernen Japanischen Literatur.* Wiesbaden, Germany: Franz Steiner Verlag, 1981.

Hodgart, Matthew. *Satire.* New York: McGraw-Hill, World University Press, 1973.

Honda Shūgo. *Monogatari: sengo bungakushi* (A Narrative: The History of Postwar Literature). Shinchōsha, 1966.

Ienaga Saburo. *The Pacific War 1931–1945.* Translated by Frank Baldwin. New York: Pantheon, 1978.

Iizawa Tadasu. *Buki to shite no warai* (Laughter as a Weapon). Iwanami Shinsho, 1977.

Ikeda Hiroshi. *Nihon bungaku no warai* (Laughter in Japanese Literature). Wakō Sensho, 1977.

Inoue Hisashi. *Parodi shigan* (Volunteering for Parody). Chūō Kōronsha, 1979.

Iwamoto Yoshio. "The 'Mad' World of Ōe Kenzaburo." *Review of Teach Us to Outgrow Our Madness*, by Ōe Kenzaburo. *Journal of the Association of Teachers of Japanese*, 14, 1 (April 1979):66–83.

Jackson, Earl, Jr. "Toward a Phenomenology of Ōe Kenzaburo: Self, World, and the Intermediating Microcosm." *Transactions of the International Conference of Orientalists in Japan* 25 (May 1980), Tōhōgakkai, pp. 47–59.

Janes, Regina. *Gabriel García Márquez: Revolutions in Wonderland.* Columbia: University of Missouri Press, 1981.

Jung, C. G. and C. Kerényi. *Essays on a Science of Mythology.* Translated by R. F. C. Hull. Princeton: Princeton University Press, 1969.

Kern, Edith. "Introduction." In *Sartre.* Edited by Edith Kern. Englewood Cliffs, N.J.: Prentice-Hall, 1962, pp. 1–14.

Kim Chi Ha. *Cry of the People and Other Poems.* Hayama, Japan: Autumn Press, 1974.

————— *From the Darkness*: *Poems.* Kingston, R.I.: George Knowlton, 197?

————— *The Golden Crowned Jesus and Other Writings.* Edited by Chong Sun Kim and Shelley Killen. Maryknoll, N.Y.: Orbis Books, 1978.

————— *The Middle Hour*; *Selected Poems of Kim Chi Ha.* Translated by David R. McCann. Sanfordville, N.Y.: Human Rights Publishing Group, 1980.

————— *Torture Road . . . 1974.* Translated by Chong Sun Kim and Shelley Killen. Kingston, R.I.: George Knowlton, 1976.

Kristeva, Julia. *Desire in Language: A Semiotic Approach to Literature and Art.* Translated by Thomas Gora, Alice Jardine, and Leon S. Roudiez. New York: Columbia University Press, 1980.

Lemon, Lee T. and Marion J. Reis, eds. and trans. *Russian Formalist Criticism: Four Essays.* Lincoln: University of Nebraska Press, 1965.

Lippit, Noriko Mizuta. *Reality and Fiction in Modern Japanese Literature.* Armonk, N.Y.: M. E. Sharpe, 1980.

Lotman, Iu. M. *Lectures on Structural Poetics, Theory of Verse.* Providence, R.I.: Brown University Slavic Reprint V, 1968.

————— *The Structure of the Artistic Text.* Translated by Ronald Vroon. Michigan Slavic Contributions, No. 7. Ann Arbor: University of Michigan.

MacAdam, Alfred J. *Modern Latin American Narratives: The Dreams of Reason.* Chicago: University of Chicago Press, 1977.

Mailer, Norman. *Advertisements for Myself.* New York: G. P. Putnam's Sons, 1959.

Makarius, Laura. "Ritual Clowns and Symbolic Behavior." *Diogenes* 69 (1970): 44–73.

Mishima Yukio. *Runaway Horses.* Translated by Michael Gallagher. New York: Knopf, 1973.

Miyoshi Masao. *Accomplices of Silence: The Modern Japanese Novel.* Berkeley: University of California Press, 1974.

Myerhoff, Barbara G. "Return to Wirikuta: Ritual Reversal and Symbolic Continuity on the Peyote Hunt of the Huichol Indians." In *The Reversible World: Symbolic Inversion in Art and Society.* Edited by Barbara A. Babcock. Ithaca: Cornell University Press, 1978, pp. 225–39.

Olson, Elder. *The Theory of Comedy.* Bloomington: Indiana University Press, 1975.

Ōoka Shohei. *Kataku no hito* (The Sufferer). Shinchōsha, 1975.

——— *Fires on the Plain* (Nobi). Translated by Ivan Morris. New York: Knopf, 1957.

Poirier, Richard. *Norman Mailer.* New York: Viking, 1972.

Radin, Paul. *The Trickster.* New York: Greenwood, 1975.

Richter, Frederick. "Circles of Shame: 'Sheep' by Ōe Kenzaburo." *Studies in Short Fiction* 11 (Fall 1974):409–15.

Seidensticker, Edward. "The 'Pure' and the 'In-Between' in Modern Japanese Theories of the Novel." In his *This Country, Japan.* New York: Kodansha International, 1979, pp. 98–111.

Shiga Naoya. *A Dark Night's Passing.* Translated by Edwin McClellan. New York: Kōdansha International, 1976.

Shukman, Ann. *Literature and Semiotics: A Study of the Writing of Yu M. Lotman.* New York: North-Holland Publishing Company, 1977.

Sibley, William F. "Naturalism in Japanese Literature." *Harvard Journal of Asiatic Studies* 28 (1968):157–69.

Todorov, Tzvetan. "The Categories of Literary Narrative." *Papers on Language and Literature* (1980):3–36.

Todorov, Tzvetan. *The Fantastic: A Structural Approach to a Literary Genre.* Translated by Richard Howard. Ithaca: Cornell University Press, 1975.

——— *The Poetics of Prose.* Translated by Richard Howard with a new Foreword by Jonathan Culler. Ithaca: Cornell University Press, 1977.

Tsuruta Kinya. "Akutagawa Ryunosuke and I-Novelists." *Monumenta Nipponica* 25, 1–2 (1970):13–27.

Turner, Victor. *The Ritual Process: Structure and Anti-Structure.* Ithaca: Cornell University Press, 1969.

——— *Dramas, Fields, and Metaphors.* Ithaca: Cornell Unviersity Press, 1974.

——— "Frame, Flow and Reflection: Ritual and Drama as Public Liminality." *Japanese Journal of Religious Studies* 6, 4 (December 1979): 469–99.

——— "Myth and Symbol." *International Encyclopedia of the Social Sciences.* 1963.

Twain, Mark. *The Adventures of Huckleberry Finn.* New York: W. W. Norton, 1977.

Ueda, Makoto. *Matsuo Basho.* New York: Twayne Publishers, 1970.

Vonnegut, Kurt. *Palm Sunday.* New York: Delacorte Press, 1981.

Walker, Janet A. *The Japanese Novel of the Meiji Period and the Ideal of Individualism.* Princeton: Princeton University Press, 1979.

Wicks, Ulrich. "The Nature of Picaresque Narrative." *PMLA* 89 (1974): 240–49.

Wilson, Michiko N. "Ōe's Obsessive Metaphor, Mori the Idiot Son: Toward the Imagination of Satire, Regeneration, and Grotesque Realism." *The Journal of Japanese Studies* 7, 1 (Winter 1981):25–52.

Yamaguchi Masao. *Bunka to ryōgisei* (Culture and Ambivalence). Iwanami Shoten, 1975.

Yoshida Sanroku. "Kenzaburo Ōe: A New World of Imagination." *Comparative Literature Studies* 22, 1 (Spring 1985):80–96.

Index

About the author

A graduate of Culver-Stockton College, Michiko N. Wilson received an M.A. in Japanese literature and a Ph.D. in comparative literature from the University of Texas at Austin. She has taught at the University of Texas at Austin, the University of California at Davis, and since 1977 the University of Virginia, where she is an associate professor of language and literature.

Professor Wilson has published papers on various aspects of Japanese and comparative literature and is currently working on a translation of Ōe Kenzaburo's story *The Pinch-runner Memorandum*.

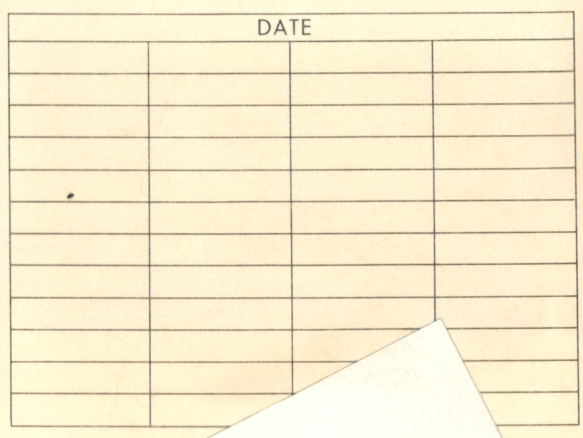